STEAD

IN YOUF

STEADFAST
IN YOUR WORD

DAILY REFLECTIONS
FROM MARTIN LUTHER

Selected & Edited by Barbara Owen

Augsburg

MINNEAPOLIS

Cover design by Sarah Gioe; cover art from Corbis
Book design by Michelle L. N. Cook; interior art from PhotoDisc

Library of Congress Cataloging-in-Publication Data
Luther, Martin, 1483-1546.
　　[Selections. English. 2001]
　　Steadfast in your word : daily reflections from Martin Luther / selected and edited by Barbara Owen.
　　p. cm.
　　Includes bibliographical references.
　　ISBN 0-8066-4422-2 (alk. paper)
　　1. Meditations. 2. Devotional calendars—Lutheran Church. 3. Lutheran Church—Prayer-books and devotions—English.
I. Owen, Barbara, 1935- II. Title.
　　BR331.E6 2001
　　242'.2—dc21   2001053378

The paper used in this publication meets the minimum requirements of American National Standard for Information Sciences—Permanence of Paper for Printed Library Materials, ANSI Z329.48-1984. ♾ ™

Manufactured in the U.S.A.   AF 9-4422

02　　03　　04　　05　　06　　1　　2　　3　　4　　5　　6　　7　　8　　9　　10

CONTENTS

Foreword   vii
Preface   ix

God the Creator   1
Knowing God   6
Incarnation   11
The Mission of Christ   16
The Cross   21
Resurrection   26
The Holy Spirit   31
The Trinity   36
Law and Gospel   41
Christian Righteousness   46
Faith Alone   51
Grace   56
Forgiveness   61
Christ in Us   66
Christian Freedom   71
Hearing God   76
Prayer   81
Worship   86
Good Works   91
Our Mission to Others   96
Vocation   101
Strength in Weakness   106
Saint and Sinner   111
Comfort   116
Hope   121
Christ the King   126

Bibliography   131
Acknowledgments   133

FOREWORD

In a "table talk" about spiritual distress, Luther disclosed his commitment to daily prayer. "Whenever I happen to be prevented by the press of duties from observing my hour of prayer," he declared, "the entire day is bad for me. Prayer helps us very much and gives us a cheerful heart, not on account of any merit in the work, but because we have spoken with God and found everything in order" (*LW* 54, p. 17).

Luther viewed daily prayer as an indispensable part of Christian formation for witness in the world. Prayer was closely tied to the catechism with its decalogue, creed, and Lord's Prayer as a spiritual survival ration in the daily struggle against sin, death, and evil. Luther had learned from the apostle Paul and St. Augustine that Christian life was an interim, the meantime between the first and second coming of Christ, at times a mean and evil time.

Luther echoed an enduring ecumenical tradition when he defined prayer as "the lifting up of heart or mind to God" (*LW* 42, p. 25). The most influential medieval theologian, Thomas Aquinas, offered the same definition of prayer. But because prayer had become a work of merit in the late medieval church, Luther insisted that prayer, like doctrine, liturgy, and ethics, be an expression of faith in Christ alone. In prayer, one should give thanks for what God did in Christ and one should petition Christ to be present through the Holy Spirit as the "counselor" who consoles and strengthens the church in the world (John 14:26). Luther, therefore, saw prayer normed by the fundamental biblical insight that Christ is the only mediator of salvation without any human merit, including the work of prayer.

Barbara Owen offers an attractive collection of Luther's writings, highlighting particular themes and concerns. This collection may help readers to begin a life of meditation and prayer and so to break new spiritual ground for a doxological life with God and with each other as the people of God on the way from earthly struggle to eternal peace.

—Eric W. Gritsch, Director
Institute for Luther Studies
Gettysburg Lutheran Seminary

PREFACE

THE MEDITATIONS HAVE ALL BEEN TAKEN FROM THE AMERICAN Edition of *Luther's Works*, abbreviated here as *LW*. The *LW* volume and page numbers for each meditation are noted beneath each page of meditations. The name of the volume is noted, as in Lectures on Romans, or, if the volume is a collection of documents, a particular document may be noted, such as "Fourteen Consolations."

The dates for the selections, also noted, are taken from the introductory material in the various volumes of *Luther's Works*. They are included here so the reader can know the approximate time in Luther's life that he wrote or spoke the material.

The Scripture texts heading the meditations are taken from the New Revised Standard Version Bible (NRSV) unless another translation is needed to fit Luther's use of the text in the meditation. Occasionally, Luther's rendering of the text is used where he has made explicit reference to words found in his translation but not in the NRSV. In the four hundred years since Luther, new discoveries about the biblical text have led the translators of the NRSV to render some passages quite differently from the way in which Luther read them. Yet many passages are remarkably similar. Scripture included in the body of the meditations is excerpted as found in the *LW* volumes. Luther often references several verses of Scripture while commenting on another.

Because Luther wrote extensively and sometimes redundantly with the tendency to go off on tangents, some selections have been abridged to delete excess material. Many have been reworked for easier reading by dividing Luther's very long sentences and paragraphs. Occasionally some paraphrasing has been necessary to make the excerpt clear in itself. However, great care has been taken not to change Luther's meaning but simply to restructure the commentary materials so that they have the flow of meditations.

"Thee" and "thou" have usually been changed to "you," and inclusive language has been used. Nevertheless, because the translation from which these meditations come is an established standard text of Luther's writings in English, it did not seem wise to make all of its language inclusive.

Some of the meditations are taken from Luther's earlier writings such as the *First Lectures on the Psalms* (1513-15), volumes 10 and 11. These are from the Luther who had not yet fully experienced the transition from medieval Catholicism to a life with a gospel of grace that cannot be earned (what Luther would later call justification through faith without the works of the law). Nevertheless, they show that Luther was already thinking about grace. After lecturing on the Psalms, Luther chose to lecture on Romans (1515-16). Luther reported that he became more "skillful" after he had also lectured on Galatians and Hebrews, but Hilton C. Oswald, editor of *LW* 25, *Lectures on Romans,* writes in his introduction, "The whole series of lectures on Romans shows Luther already 'skillful' in his understanding of the righteousness of God, even though he still moves about in much of the vocabulary and the teaching forms of his predecessors distant and near." Within the context of Luther's later work reflected in other selections in this book, these early writings can be profitably read devotionally.

—Barbara Owen

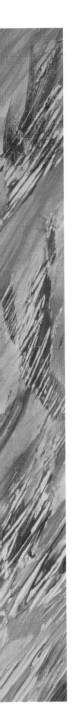

GOD THE CREATOR

In the beginning when God created
the heavens and the earth.
—Genesis 1:1

THE FIRST ARTICLE OF THE APOSTLES' CREED TEACHES THAT GOD is the Father, the creator of heaven and earth. What is this? What do these words mean? The meaning is that I should believe that I am God's creature, that he has given to me body, soul, good eyes, reason, a good wife, children, fields, meadows, pigs, and cows, and besides this, he has given to me the four elements, water, fire, air, and earth. Thus this article teaches that you do not have your life of yourself, not even a hair. I would not even have a pig's ear, if God had not created it for me. Everything that exists is comprehended in that little word "creator." Therefore, everything you have, however small it may be, remember this when you say "creator," even if you set great store by it. Do not let us think that we have created ourselves, as the proud princes do.

"Ten Sermons on the Catechism" (1528)
LW 51, 162-63

Then the LORD God formed man from the dust
of the ground, and breathed into his nostrils the breath
of life; and the man became a living being.
—Genesis 2:7

 believe that he has given to me my life, my five senses, reason, spouse, and children. None of these do I have of myself. God is the "creator," that is, God has given everything, body and soul, including every member of the body. But if everything is the gift of God, then you owe it to him to serve him with all these things and praise and thank him, since he has given them and still preserves them. But, I ask you, how many are there in the world who understand this word "creator"? For nobody serves him. We sin against God with all our members, one after another, with wife, children, house, home.

In short, the first article of the Apostles' Creed teaches creation, the second redemption, the third sanctification. The creation, it teaches, means that I believe that God has given to me body, life, reason, and all that I possess. These things I have not of myself, that I may not become proud. I cannot either give them to myself or keep them by myself. But why has he given them to you and what do you think he gave them to you for? It is in order that you should praise him and thank him. There are many who say these words, "I believe in God the Father," but do not understand what these words mean.

"Ten Sermons on the Catechism"(1528)
LW 51, 163-64

For though the LORD is high,
he regards the lowly.
—Psalm 138:6a

Just as God in the beginning of creation made the world out of nothing, whence he is called the Creator and the Almighty, so his manner of working continues unchanged. Even now and to the end of the world, all his works are such that out of that which is nothing, worthless, despised, wretched, and dead, he makes that which is something, precious, honorable, blessed, and living. Therefore his eyes look only upon the lowly (Ps. 138:6). The eyes of the world and of men, on the contrary, look only above them and are lifted up with pride.

But to God alone belongs that sort of seeing that looks upon the lowly with their need and misery, and is near to all that are in the depths; as St. Peter says (1 Peter 5:5): "God opposes the proud but gives grace to the humble." And this is the source of believers' love and praise of God. For no one can praise God without first loving him. No one can love him unless he makes himself known to them in the most lovable and intimate fashion. And he can make himself known only through those words of his which he reveals in us, and which we feel and experience within ourselves. But where there is this experience, namely, that he is a God who looks upon the lowly and helps only the poor, despised, afflicted, miserable, forsaken, and those who are nothing, there a hearty love for him is born.

3

Commentary on "The Magnificat" [Luke 1:46-55] (1521)
LW 21, 299-300

Then God spoke all these words:"I am the LORD your God."
—Exodus 20:1-2a

I take the risk of placing my confidence only in the one, invisible, inscrutable, and only God, who created heaven and earth and who alone is superior to all creation. Again, I am not terrified by all the wickedness of the devil and his cohorts because God is superior to them all.

I would believe in God not a bit less if everyone were to forsake me and persecute me. I would believe in God no less if I were poor, unintelligent, uneducated, despised, or lacking in everything. I believe no less though I am a sinner. For this manner of faith will of necessity rise over all that does or does not exist, over sin and virtue and all else, thus depending purely and completely upon God as the First Commandment enjoins me to do.

I do not ask for any sign from God to put him to the test. I trust in him steadfastly, no matter how long he may delay, prescribing neither a goal, nor a time, nor a measure, nor a way for God to respond to me, but leaving all to his divine will in a free, honest, and genuine faith.

If he is the Creator of heaven and earth and Lord over everything, who, then, could deprive me of anything, or work me harm (Rom. 8:31)? Yes, how can it be otherwise than that all things work for good for me (Rom. 8:28) if the God, whom all creation obeys and depends upon, is well intentioned toward me?

"Personal Prayer Book"(1522)
LW 43, 25-26

"Where, O death, is your victory?
Where, O death, is your sting?"
—1 Corinthians 15:55

When Isaac's throat was about to be cut, he thought: "Into thy hands I commit my spirit (Ps. 31:5). I shall not die, but I shall live; and I shall return, because God will not lie. I am the son of the promise. Therefore I must beget children, even if heaven collapses." There was a great light of faith in that young man. He believed in God the Creator, who calls into existence the things that do not exist (Rom. 4:17), and commands the ashes that are not Isaac to be Isaac. For he who believes that God is the Creator, who makes all things out of nothing, must of necessity conclude that therefore God can raise the dead.

But all this has its source in the first of the Ten Commandments; for in it is contained the doctrine of faith and of the resurrection of the dead. "I, the almighty creator of heaven and earth, am your God; that is, you must live the life I am living." If he were speaking these words to oxen, they would live forever. But they are said to us—to us, I say. He does not say to them: "You must eat chaff, wheat, and grass." No, he says: "I am your God."

Furthermore, to be God means to deliver from all evils that burden us, such as sin, hell, death; for in this manner the prophets regarded and interpreted these words. The heathen know God solely as the Creator; but in the First Commandment you will find Christ, life, victory over death, and the resurrection of the dead into eternal life, and finally the entire Old and New Testaments. But only those who have the Holy Spirit and pay attention to what God says and does see this.

Lectures on Genesis (1539-40)
LW 4, 119-20

5

KNOWING GOD

"Believe in God, believe also in me."
—John 14:1b

CHRIST WANTS TO SAY HERE: "YOU HAVE HEARD THAT YOU MUST trust in God. But I want to show you where you will truly find him, lest your thoughts create an idol bearing the name of God. If you want to believe in God, then believe in me. If you want to apply your faith and your confidence properly, that it may not be amiss or false, then direct it toward me, for in me the entire Godhead dwells perfectly."

Later Christ declares (John 14:6, 9): "I am the Way, the Truth, and the Life. He who has seen me has seen the Father. He who hears me hears the Father. Therefore if you want to be sure to meet God, take hold of him in me and through me."

Repeatedly in the Gospels Christ declares that he was sent by the Father. He says and does nothing of his own accord, but states that it is the Father's order and command to all the world to believe Christ as God himself. Thus no one dare adopt another person or means to apprehend God than this one Christ. He assures us that if we rely on him, we will not encounter an idol, as the others do who resort to other ways to deal with God.

It is certain that those who bypass the person of Christ never find the true God. Because God is fully in Christ, where he places himself for us, no effort to deal with God without and apart from Christ on the strength of human thoughts and devotion will be successful.

Whoever would travel the right road and not go astray with his faith, let them begin where God says and where he wants to be found, in this man—Jesus Christ.

Sermons on the Gospel of St. John (1537-38)
LW 24, 17, 23

Have mercy on me, O God, according to your steadfast love;
according to your abundant mercy blot out my transgressions.
—Psalm 51:1

David is talking to the God of his fathers—the God who promised. The people of Israel did not have a God who was viewed "absolutely." Human weakness cannot help being crushed by the majesty of the absolute God, as Scripture reminds us over and over. Let no one, therefore, interpret David as speaking with the absolute God.

He is speaking with God as he is dressed and clothed in his word and promises, so that from the name "God" we cannot exclude Christ, whom God promised to Adam and the other patriarchs. We must take hold of this God, not naked but clothed and revealed in his word. Otherwise certain despair will crush us.

This distinction must always be made between the Prophets who speak with God and the pagans. Pagans speak with God outside his word and promises, according to the thoughts of their own hearts. But the Prophets speak with God as he is clothed and revealed in his promises and word. This God, clothed in such a kind appearance and dressed in his promises—this God we can grasp and look at with joy and trust. The absolute God, on the other hand, is like an iron wall against which we cannot bump without destroying ourselves. Therefore Satan is busy day and night, making us run to the naked God so that we forget his promises and blessings shown in Christ and think about God and the judgment of God.

But David speaks with the God of his fathers, with the God whose promises he knows and whose mercy and grace he has felt. He could depend on God's promises as he prayed because the promises include Christ.

Commentary on "Psalm 51" (1532)
LW 12, 312-13

7

For when God made his promise to Abraham,
he made a vow to do what he had promised.
—Hebrews 6:13a (TEV)

Chrysostom says: ". . . by means of these words (the apostle) comforts . . . by showing God's customary way of doing things. . . . It is not his custom to fulfill his promises swiftly but to do so after a long time."Therefore those who want to serve God must learn to know his will and his custom. For who can serve a master whom they do not know?

But to learn to know God in nature the way the philosophers learned to know his power and his essence (Rom. 1:20) is not enough. One must learn to know what his will or what his plan is.

This he shows in his commandments, as Psalm 103:7 states: "He made known his ways to Moses and his will to the children of Israel." But no one understands his commandments, either, unless illumined anew from above. "For who among mortals will be able to know the counsel of God, or who will be able to think what God's will is?" (Wisd. 9:13). Likewise (1 Cor. 2:11, 10): "The things of God no one knows but the Spirit of God. But God has revealed them to us through his spirit."

And so we read in Psalm 119 "Teach me," "Instruct me," "Give me understanding." With all these words not only God's essence but especially his will is commended. Therefore those who presume to grasp Holy Scripture and the Law of God with their own intellect and to understand them by their own effort are exceedingly in error. For this is the source of heresies and godless dogmas, for they approach, not as receptive pupils but as bustling teachers.

"Lectures on Hebrews" (1517)
LW 29, 185-86

*"I have made known to you everything
that I heard from my Father."
—John 15:15b*

These are beautiful and comforting words. Christ says to us: "If you want to know the Father's will and thought in heaven, you have all the information right here, for I have told you everything." A Christian can arrive at this definite conclusion and say: "God be praised, I know everything that God wants and has at heart. Nothing that serves my salvation is concealed from me."

Christ is not saying that we are to have an answer to every question, but that we have God's whole plan and counsel for us. If you want to be certain what God in heaven thinks of you, you must not seclude yourself, retire into some nook, and brood about it or seek the answer in your works or in your contemplation. Banish all this from your heart. Give ear solely to the words of this Christ, for everything is revealed in him.

9

And here he declares: "I was sent to you by My Father that I might shed my blood and die for you. As a token of this you have Baptism and the Sacrament, and I ask you to believe this. Here you have all that I know and have heard from the Father. The Father has no other plan and intention toward you than to save you if you have Christ and faith. From this you see how I love you, and what friendship, glory, joy, consolation, and assurance you have from me. You cannot attain this anywhere else, either in heaven or on earth."

Sermons on the Gospel of St. John (1537)
LW 24, 257

But in these last days he has spoken to us by a Son,
whom he appointed heir of all things,
through whom he also created the worlds.
——Hebrews 1:2

The writer describes the same Christ as the Son of Man and the Son of God. For the words "He was appointed the heir of all things" are properly applicable to him because of his humanity. But the words "the worlds were made through him" apply to him because of his divinity.

One should also note that he mentions the humanity of Christ before he mentions his divinity, in order that he may establish the well-known rule that one learns to know God in faith. For the humanity is that holy ladder of ours, mentioned in Gen. 28:12, by which we ascend to the knowledge of God.

Therefore Christ says: "No one comes to the Father but by me" (John 14:6). And again: "I am the door" (John 10:7). He who wants to ascend advantageously to the love and knowledge of God should abandon the human metaphysical rules concerning knowledge of the divinity and apply himself first to the humanity of Christ. For it is exceedingly godless temerity that, where God has humiliated himself in order to become recognizable, mortals seek for themselves another way by following the counsels of their own natural capacity. For Christ is the image of the invisible God, as it says in Col. 1:15.

"Lectures on Hebrews"(1517)
LW 29, 110-11

10

INCARNATION

And the Word became flesh and lived among us.
—John 1:14a

CHRIST MUST BE TRUE GOD; OTHERWISE WE ARE DAMNED forever. But in his humanity he must also be a true and natural Son of the Virgin Mary, from whom he inherited flesh and blood as any other child does from its mother. He was conceived of the Holy Spirit according to Luke 1:35. However, Mary, the pure virgin, had to contribute of her seed and of the natural blood that coursed from her heart. From her he derived everything, except sin, that a child naturally and normally receives from its mother. This we must believe if we are not to be lost. If, as the Manichaeans [a heretical group in the third and fourth centuries] allege, he is not a real and natural man, born of Mary, then he is not of our flesh and blood. Then he has nothing in common with us; then we can derive no comfort from him.

However, we do not let ourselves be troubled by the blasphemies that the devil speaks against Christ the Lord. We cling to the Scriptures of the prophets and apostles, who spoke as they were moved by the Holy Spirit. Their testimony about Christ is clear. He is our brother; we are members of his body, flesh, and bone.

To sum up, we must, first of all, have a savior who can save us from the power of sin and death. This means that he must be the true, eternal God, through whom all believers in him become righteous and are saved. But, secondly, we must have a savior who is also our brother, who is of our flesh and blood. "In the beginning was the Word"; "This Word," he added later, "became flesh."

Sermons on the Gospel of St. John (1537-40)
LW 22, 23-25

He was in the world, and the world came into being
through him; yet the world did not know him.
—*John 1:10*

The evangelist John says here that the Word—which was from eternity, coequal with the Father in power and glory, through which all things were made, and which is also the Life and the Light of humankind—assumed human nature, was born of Mary, came into the world, dwelt among people in this temporal life, became like any other human being in all things, took the physical, human form such as yours or mine, and was cumbered with all the human frailties, as St. Paul says in Phil. 2:7. This means that he ate, drank, slept, awakened, was tired, sad, and happy. He wept and laughed, hungered, thirsted, froze, and perspired. He chatted, worked, and prayed. In brief, he required the same things for life's sustenance and preservation that any other human being does. He labored and suffered as anyone else does. He experienced both fortune and misfortune. The only difference between him and all others was that he was sinless. Because he was also very God, he was free of sin. And yet he was the one through whom the whole world was created and made.

Sermons on the Gospel of St. John (1537-40)
LW 22, 73

The spirit of the Lord GOD is upon me,
because the LORD has anointed me;
he has sent me to bring good news to the oppressed.
—*Isaiah 61:1a*

I t is Christ who is defined here as the one to whom the office of the word has been committed. Be content with him, the God incarnate. Then you will remain in peace and safety, and you will know God. Cast off speculations about divine glory; stay with Christ crucified, whom Paul and others preach. But those who immerse themselves in their own speculations about the divine, for example, why God spares so many unbelievers and condemns so many, they are plunged into confusion or despair because of such speculations. Because Christ and his office are here set forth, we must be content with that description.

It is because of his humanity and his incarnation that Christ becomes sweet to us, and through him God becomes sweet to us. Let us therefore begin to ascend step by step from Christ's crying in his swaddling clothes up to his passion. Then we shall easily know God. I am saying this so that you do not begin to contemplate God from the top, but start with the weak elements. We should busy ourselves completely with treating, knowing, and considering this man. Then you will know that he is the way, the truth, and the life (John 14:6). So he set forth his weakness that we may approach him with confidence.

13

Lectures on Isaiah (1527-30)
LW 17, 330-31

*"For my eyes have seen your salvation, which you have
prepared in the presence of all peoples, a light for revelation
to the Gentiles and for glory to your people Israel."
And the child's father and mother were amazed
at what was being said about him.*
—Luke 2:30-33

T he evangelist has established here a distinguishing mark:
he does not mention Joseph and Mary by name; he calls
them father and mother, in order to point out the spiritual meaning. Who, then, are Christ's spiritual father and mother?
He himself names his spiritual mother in Mark 3:34-35: "He who
does the will of my father, that one is my brother, my sister, and my
mother." St. Paul calls himself a father in 1 Corinthians 4:15. Thus
the Christian church, that is, all believing persons, is Christ's spiritual mother, and all apostles and teachers of the people, who
preach the gospel, are his spiritual father. As often as a person
becomes a believer, Christ is born of them. These are the people
who marvel over the statements of the prophets, that they apply so
nicely and accurately to Christ, speak of him so gloriously, and bear
witness to the whole gospel so masterfully. There is no greater joy
in this life than to see and experience this in Scripture.

*Sermon on "The Gospel for the Sunday after Christmas,
Luke 2[:33-40]" (1522)
LW 52, 107*

14

Jesus said to him, "I am the way, and the truth, and the life.
No one comes to the Father except through me."
—John 14:6

Whenever you consider the doctrine of justification and wonder how or where or in what condition to find a God who justifies or accepts sinners, then you must know that there is no other God than this man Jesus Christ. Take hold of him; cling to him with all your heart, and spurn all speculation about the Divine Majesty; for whoever investigates the majesty of God will be consumed by his glory. Christ himself says, "I am the way . . ." (John 14:6).

You must pay attention only to this man, who presents himself to us as the Mediator and says: "Come to me, all who labor . . ." (Matt. 11:28). When you do this, you will see the love, the goodness, and the sweetness of God. You will see his wisdom, his power, and his majesty sweetened and mitigated to your ability to stand it. And in this lovely picture you will find everything, as Paul says to the Colossians 2: "In Christ are hid all the treasures of wisdom and knowledge"; and "In him the whole fullness of deity dwells bodily." The world does not see this, because it looks at him only as a man in his weakness.

15

That is why Paul makes such a frequent practice of linking Jesus Christ with God the Father, to teach us what is the true Christian religion. It does not begin at the top, as all other religions do; it begins at the bottom. You must run directly to the manger and the mother's womb, embrace this Infant and Virgin's Child in your arms, and look at him—born, being nursed, growing up, going about in human society, teaching, dying, rising again, ascending above all the heavens, and having authority over all things.

Lectures on Galatians (1535)
LW 26, 29-30

THE MISSION OF CHRIST

"The Son of Man came not to be served but to serve,
and to give his life as a ransom for many."
—Matthew 20:28

MAY YOU EVER CHERISH AND TREASURE THIS THOUGHT. CHRIST IS made a servant to sin, yea, a bearer of sin, and the lowliest and most despised person. He destroys all sin by himself and says: "I came not to be served but to serve" (Matt. 20:28). There is no greater bondage than that of sin; and there is no greater service than that displayed by the Son of God, who becomes the servant of all, no matter how poor, wretched, or despised they may be, and bears their sins.

It would be spectacular and amazing, prompting all the world to open ears and eyes, mouth and nose in uncomprehending wonderment, if some king's son were to appear in a beggar's home to nurse him in his illness, wash off his filth, and do everything else the beggar would have to do. Would this not be profound humility? Any spectator or any beneficiary of this honor would feel impelled to admit that he had seen or experienced something unusual and extraordinary, something magnificent.

And yet the love of the Son of God for us is of such magnitude that the greater the filth and stench of our sins, the more he befriends us, the more he cleanses us, relieving us of all our misery and of the burden of all our sins and placing them upon His own back.

Whenever the devil declares: "You are a sinner!" Christ interposes: "I will reverse the order; I will be a sinner, and you are to go scotfree." Who can thank our God enough for this mercy?

Sermons on the Gospel of St. John (1537-40)
LW 22, 166-67

"Yet even if I do judge, my judgment is valid; for it is not I alone who judge, but I and the Father who sent me."
—John 8:16

T o be sure, Christ's primary mission is not to judge but to help. This is his real office, and this we must bear in mind. In John 3:17 Christ said: "For God sent the Son into the world, not to condemn the world, but that the world might be saved through him." This is the chief function of Christ, and to this end he came into the world. But if some will not accept this or submit to him who would help, then is it Christ's fault that they who reject life are given over to death?

In Genesis 22:18 it is written of Christ: "In your seed shall all the nations of the earth be blessed." This is to be his title and his office, namely, to bless, to help, to counsel. Here we find the sweet word "bless," help. He is to be a comforting preacher, a friendly man and helper, who will spare no effort and do nothing but teach and work, help and bless. With him is pure help and consolation. Yet these same words include condemnation, judgment, and sentence. Wherever a blessing is rejected, there a curse follows. Those who will not have help and comfort must take damnation. Those who will not be well must remain sick. Those who will not go to heaven must go to hell. Although it is not part of Christ's office to consign to hell, to curse, or to condemn, but to help and rescue, it is equally true that those who scorn this help must remain in hell.

17

Sermons on the Gospel of St. John (1530-32)
LW 23, 338-39

To whom then will you compare me,
or who is my equal? says the Holy One.
—Isaiah 40:25

 od bids us lift up our head. He sets forth his word and with it gives himself to us, so that all things are ours, and we, on the other hand, may cast our weakness off on Christ. If I am a sinner, Christ is righteous; if I am poor, Christ is rich; if I am foolish, Christ is wise; if I am a captive, Christ is present to set me free; if I am forsaken, Christ takes me to himself; if I am cast down, Christ consoles me; if I am weary, Christ refreshes me. Finally, he pours himself out for me altogether. Should not these things console me, for they cannot be compared with anything for value?

Lectures on Isaiah (1527-30)
LW 17, 28

Here is my servant, whom I uphold, my chosen,
in whom my soul delights . . .
—Isaiah 42:1a

hese are words of demonstration, as if he were pointing to something worth seeing. "If you want to know and be wise, look to this Christ, the doctor and the one in charge and up and doing. Him I have put in charge. Keep your eye on him, observe what he does, says, and teaches, because he is my servant." This was not written for Christ's sake but for ours, so that we may be sure about his work and teaching and may have certainty about the emptiness of our idolatry. Nobody understands these things unless he believes. You must believe that Christ is a servant as stated in this passage. Here we have the most reliable voice, and this teaching is for us. But we see from experience that nothing is more absurd to the wisdom of the flesh than Christ, the servant, and his word. All are offended because of him. All of us want to be God's servants while we please ourselves.

But for Christ, here, in the time of his earthly life, he will be servant. After death he will be Lord. In his life he will be the most prudent servant.

Lectures on Isaiah (1527-30)
LW 17, 60-61, 216

For Jesus is the one who leads them to salvation.
—Hebrews 2:10 (TEV)

od the Father made Christ to be the sign and idea in order that those who adhere to him by faith might be transformed into the same image (2 Cor. 3:18) and thus be drawn away from the images of the world. Therefore Isaiah says: "The Lord will raise an ensign for the nations, and will assemble the outcasts of Israel," and "The Root of Jesse, which stands as an ensign to the peoples; him shall the nations seek" (Isaiah 11:12, 10).

This gathering together of the children of God is similar to what happens when the government arranges a spectacle to which the citizens flock. They leave their work and their homes and fix their attention on it alone. Thus through the Gospel as through a spectacle exhibited to the whole world (cf. 2 Cor. 4:9) Christ attracts all people by the knowledge and contemplation of himself and draws them away from the things to which they have clung in the world.

20

In this way Christ is the cause and leader of salvation, for he draws and leads his children to glory through him. One would commonly say that Christ is the instrument and the means by which God leads his children. For God does not compel believers to salvation by force and fear, but by this pleasing spectacle of his mercy and love he moves and draws through love all those whom he will save.

"Lectures on Hebrews"(1517-18)
LW 29, 132

THE CROSS

"Whoever does not take up the cross and follow me
is not worthy of me."
—*Matthew 10:38*

WE MUST NOTE IN THE FIRST PLACE THAT CHRIST BY HIS suffering not only saved us from the devil, death, and sin, but also that his suffering is an example, which we are to follow in our suffering. Though our suffering and cross should never be so exalted that we think we can be saved by it or earn the least merit through it, nevertheless we should suffer after Christ, that we may be conformed to him. For God has appointed that we should not only believe in the crucified Christ, but also be crucified with him, as he clearly shows in the above Scripture and in many places in the Gospels: "If they have called the master of the house Beelzebul, how much more will they malign those of his household" (Matt. 10:25). Therefore every Christian must be aware that suffering will not fail to come.

Beyond this, it should be the kind of suffering which we have not chosen ourselves, as the fanatics choose their own suffering. It should be the kind of suffering that, if it were possible, we would gladly be rid of, suffering visited upon us by the devil or the world. Then what is needed is to hold fast and submit oneself to it, as I have said, namely, that one know that we must suffer, in order that we may thus be conformed to Christ, and that it cannot be otherwise, that everyone must have his cross and suffering.

"Sermon on Cross and Suffering, Preached at Coburg"(1530)
LW 51, 198-99

By his great mercy he has given us a new birth into a living
hope through the resurrection of Jesus Christ from the dead,
and into an inheritance that is imperishable, undefiled, and
unfading. . . . In this you rejoice, even if now for a little while
you have had to suffer various trials.
—1 Peter 1:3b-4a, 6

The cause of our suffering is the same as that for which all the saints have suffered from the beginning. Of course the whole world must bear witness that we are not suffering because of public scandal or vice, such as adultery, fornication, murder, and the like. Rather we suffer because we hold to the Word of God, preach it, hear it, learn it, and practice it. And because this is the cause of our suffering, so let it always be; we have the same promise and the same cause for suffering, which all the saints have always had. We, too, can comfort ourselves with the same promise and cling to it in our suffering and tribulation, as is highly necessary.

So in our suffering we should so act that we give our greatest attention to the promise, in order that our cross and affliction may be turned to good, to something that we could never have asked or thought. And this is precisely the thing that makes a difference between the Christian's suffering and afflictions and those of all other people. For they also have their afflictions, cross, and misfortune, just as they also have their times when they can sit in the rose garden and employ their good fortune and their goods as they please. But when they run into affliction and suffering, they have nothing to comfort them, for they do not have the mighty promises and confidence in God that Christians have. Therefore they cannot comfort themselves with the assurance that God will help them to bear the affliction, much less can they count on it that he will turn their affliction and suffering to good.

"Sermon on Cross and Suffering, Preached at Coburg" (1530)
LW 51, 200-1

For many live as enemies of the cross of Christ; I have often
told you of them, and now I tell you even with tears.
—Philippians 3:18

This is clear: Those who do not know Christ do not know
God hidden in suffering. Therefore they prefer works to
suffering, glory to the cross, strength to weakness, wisdom to folly, and in general, good to evil. These are the people whom the apostle calls "enemies of the cross of Christ" for they hate the cross and suffering and love works and the glory of works. Thus they call the good of the cross evil and the evil of a deed good. God can be found only in suffering and the cross, as has already been said. Therefore the friends of the cross say that the cross is good and works are evil, for through the cross works are dethroned and the old Adam, who is especially edified by works, is crucified. It is impossible for believers not to be puffed up by their good works unless they have first been deflated and destroyed by suffering and evil until they know that they are worthless and that their works are not theirs but God's.

"Heidelberg Disputation"(1518)
LW 31, 53

"My God, my God, why have you forsaken me?"
—Matthew 27:46b

 ou must look at sin only within the picture of grace. The picture of grace is nothing else but that of Christ on the cross and of all his dear saints.

How is that to be understood? Grace and mercy are there where Christ on the cross takes your sin from you, bears it for you, and destroys it. To believe this firmly, to keep it before your eyes and not to doubt it, means to view the picture of Christ and to engrave it in yourself. Here sins are never sins, for here they are overcome and swallowed up in Christ. He takes your death upon himself and strangles it so that it may not harm you, if you believe that he does it for you and see your death in him and not in yourself. Likewise, he also takes your sins upon himself and overcomes them with his righteousness out of sheer mercy, and if you believe that, your sins will never work you harm.

So then, gaze at the heavenly picture of Christ, who descended into hell (1 Pet. 3:19) for your sake and was forsaken by God as one eternally damned when he spoke the words on the cross, "Eli, Eli, lama sabachthani!"—"My God, my God, why hast thou forsaken me?" (Matt. 27:46). In that picture your hell is defeated and your uncertain election is made sure. If you concern yourself solely with that and believe that it was done for you, you will surely be preserved in this same faith. Never, therefore, let this be erased from your vision. Seek yourself only in Christ and not in yourself and you will find yourself in him eternally.

"A Sermon on Preparing to Die"(1519)
LW 42, 104-6

He will drink from the stream by the path.
—Psalm 110:7a

In this life, the prophet says, he will "drink from the brook [stream]"; that is he will suffer and die. By "drink" or "cup" Scripture means any sort of torture, misery, and suffering just as Christ prayed in the garden, where he sweat blood (Luke 22:44) and said (Matt. 26:39): "Dear Father, if it is possible, remove this cup from me. But if it cannot be otherwise but that I drink it, thy will be done."

But here we do not have the simple expression "drink of the cup," as in other places. "He will drink from the brook" is intended to show that he will not feel ordinary or small pains and misery; but he will bear or endure the greatest, the most bitter and cruel pain and torture, and will die a most contemptible death. For the word "torrent" refers to a strong and fast-flowing stream or brook, which, when it is swollen from heavy rains, tears irresistibly onward in full flood. So the suffering of Christ is not called a mere drink or cupful but means drinking up an entire stream or brook, as Psalm 42:7 also says of such suffering: "All thy waves and all thy billows have gone over me." This stream, then, is the whole world with its power. Lastly, we should mention the devil and all his hell, sin, the terror and fear of death, and whatever other miseries exist. All this came upon him; he had to drink it up and conquer.

25

Commentary on "Psalm 110" (1535)
LW 13, 345-46

RESURRECTION

[Jesus our Lord] was handed over to death for our trespasses
and was raised for our justification.
—Romans 4:25

NOW WE COME TO THE RESURRECTION OF CHRIST, TO THE DAY OF
Easter. After a person has contemplated the passion and cross of
Christ and has thus become aware of his sin and is terrified in his
heart, he must watch that sin does not remain in his conscience,
for this would lead to sheer despair.

You cast your sins from yourself and onto Christ when you
firmly believe that his wounds and sufferings are your sins, to be
borne and paid for by him, as we read in Isaiah 53:6: "The Lord
has laid on him the iniquity of us all." St. Peter says, "in his body
has he borne our sins on the wood of the cross" (1 Pet. 2:24).
You must stake everything on these and similar verses. But if you
behold your sin resting on Christ and see it overcome by his resurrection, and then boldly believe this, even it is dead and nulli-
fied. Sin cannot remain on Christ, for it is swallowed up in his
resurrection. Now you see no wounds, no pain in him, and no
sign of sin. Thus St. Paul declares that "Christ died for our sins
and rose for our justification." That is to say, in his suffering
Christ makes our sins known and thus destroys them, but
through his resurrection he justifies us and delivers us from all
sin, if we believe this.

"A Meditation on Christ's Passion"(1519)
LW 42, 12

*We know that Christ, being raised from the dead, will never
die again; death no longer has dominion over him.*
—Romans 6:9

Behold Jesus Christ, the King of glory, rising from the
dead. Here the heart can find its supreme joy and lasting
possessions. Here there is not the slightest trace of evil,
for "Christ being risen from the dead, will not die again. Death no
longer has dominion over him." Here is that furnace of love and the
fire of God in Zion, as Isaiah says, for Christ is not only born to us,
but also given to us [Isa. 9:6]. Therefore, his resurrection and
everything that he accomplished through it are mine. In Romans
8:32 the Apostle exults in exuberant joy, "Has he not also given me
all things with him?"

What is it that he has wrought by his resurrection? He has
destroyed sin and raised up righteousness, abolished death and
restored life, conquered hell and bestowed everlasting glory on us.
These blessings are so incalculable that the human mind hardly
dares believe that they have been granted to us. I am a sinner, but I
am borne by his righteousness, which is given to me. I am unclean,
but his holiness is my sanctification, in which I ride gently. I am an
ignorant fool, but his wisdom carries me forward. I deserve condemnation, but I am set free by his redemption.

27

"Fourteen Consolations" (1520)
LW 42, 163-64

*Then the LORD replied to [Moses], "I will raise up
from them a prophet like you from among their own people;
I will put my words in the mouth of the prophet,
who shall speak to them everything I command."*
—*Deuteronomy 18:17-18*

This statement, and others like it, perpetuated the confident faith in the coming of Christ the Messiah among the Jewish people. They waited for the one who, as Moses had said in this passage, would teach them everything. In this faith they died. They were saved as well as we are, who now believe that Christ ascended to heaven and sits at the right hand of his Father, that he will raise us from the dead on the last day and make us more radiant and resplendent than the sun, that he will judge the quick and the dead, that he will save all believers, and that he will also raise the body from the grave. Although we must all die before we experience this, we are firmly persuaded and believe that it will come to pass. In this confidence we die; and by this faith we are saved, although we do not yet understand just how it will happen. But even though we do not see this, grasp it, or understand it, nonetheless we know that whoever believes will be saved.

Similarly, we take hold of eternal life by faith today, although we do not really understand what it is. We believe that one day we shall partake of it.

Sermons on the Gospel of St. John (1537-40)
LW 22, 285

I will raise them up on the last day.
—John 6:54b

ou must not judge by external appearances. You must be guided by the word, which promises and gives you everlasting life. Then you truly have eternal life.

Even though your senses tell you otherwise, this does not matter. This does not mean that you have forfeited life, for sickness, death, perils, and sin that assail you will not devour or finish you. They will have to leave you in peace. They do not weaken or kill Christ. When these all have passed and have left you constant in your faith, then you will see what you have believed.

But you retort: "The fact remains that I must die."

This makes no difference! Go ahead and die in God's name. You are still assured of eternal life; it will surely be yours. To die, to be buried, to have people tread on your grave, to be consumed by worms—all this will not matter to you. It is certain that Christ will raise you up again. For here you have his promise: "I will raise you up."

Therefore your eyes will behold what your faith so confidently relied on.

Sermons on the Gospel of St. John (1530-32)
LW 23, 131

29

. . . the hope of eternal life that God, who never lies,
promised before the ages began.
—Titus 1:2

his is also a word of confidence, because he is speaking against those who are timid and weak in faith when he says "who does not lie." For to believe that in hope one has a life that is eternal, this passes all understanding (Phil. 4:7), even that of the godly. The ungodly ridicule this proclamation when they hear it. But the godly strive to believe this, because it is the greatest of doctrines to believe in eternal life.

Thus the weak should be buoyed up with these words: "Do you not think that he will live up to what he has said?" Thus Christ gives the consolation in Luke 12:32: "Fear not, O little flock." This consolation has always been necessary for all believers; for if people look about them, they stumble at the idea of eternal life. Our primary impression is that we are sinners, but it is a sublime thing to believe that God has prepared eternal life. He raises the poor up from the dirt and leads them from sin and death; he crowns the unworthy. Thus he says in John 14:1-2: "Let not your heart be troubled. In my Father's house, do not doubt. Eternal life is promised to you. It is a grand thing, but do not fear. You are a little flock, but you should have the courage to believe; for it has pleased the Father. Besides, if dwelling places were not prepared, I would prepare them for you now."

"Lectures on Titus" (1527)
LW 29, 11-12

THE HOLY SPIRIT

"When the Spirit of truth comes, he will guide you
into all the truth; for he will not speak on his own,
but will speak whatever he hears, and he will declare
to you the things that are to come."
—John 16:13

HERE CHRIST DEFINES THE HOLY SPIRIT'S OFFICE AND POINTS out what and about what he is to teach. He constantly keeps in mind the false spirits and preachers who boastfully claim to have the Holy Spirit and allege that what they say has emanated from the Holy Spirit. There are some who speak on their own authority; that is, they evolve their message from their own reasoning or religious zeal and judgment. The Holy Spirit is not to be that kind of preacher; for he will not speak on his own authority, and his message will not be a human dream and thought like that of the preachers who speak on their own authority of things, which they have neither seen nor experienced.

"No," Christ says, "his message will have substance; it will be certain and absolute truth, for he will preach what he receives from the Father and from me. And you will be able to recognize him by the fact that he does not speak on his own authority—as the spirit of lies, the devil, and his mobs do—but will preach about what he will hear. Thus he will speak exclusively of me and will glorify me, so that the people will believe in me."

In this way Christ sets bounds for the message of the Holy Spirit himself. He is not to preach anything new or anything else than Christ and his word.

Sermons on the Gospel of St. John (1537)
LW 24, 362-63

And because you are children, God has sent the Spirit
of his Son into our hearts.
—Galatians 4:6a

We must not doubt that the Holy Spirit dwells in us. We must be sure and acknowledge that we are a "temple of the Holy Spirit" (1 Cor. 6:19). For if someone experiences love toward the Word, and if he enjoys hearing, speaking, thinking, and writing about Christ, he should know that this is not a work of human will or reason but a gift of the Holy Spirit.

And therefore we should believe that whatever we say, do, or think is pleasing to God, not on our account but on account of Christ. We are most certain that Christ is pleasing to God and that he is holy. To the extent that Christ is pleasing to God and that we cling to him, we, too, are pleasing to God and holy. Although sin still clings to our flesh, and we still fall every day, still grace is more abundant and more powerful than sin.

This inner assurance that we are in a state of grace and have the Holy Spirit is accompanied by the external signs I have mentioned: to enjoy hearing about Christ; to teach, give thanks, praise, and confess him; to do one's duty according to one's calling; to help the needy and comfort the sorrowful. By these signs we are assured and confirmed that we are in a state of grace.

Lectures on Galatians (1535)
LW 26, 376, 378-79

. . . the Spirit of his Son . . . crying, "Abba! Father!"
—Galatians 4:6

I t is a very great comfort that the Spirit of Christ, sent by God into our hearts, cries: "Abba! Father!" He helps us in our weakness and intercedes for us with sighs too deep for words. Anyone who truly believed this would not fall away in any affliction. But many things hinder this faith. Our heart was born in sin. Further, we have the innate evil in us that we doubt the favor of God toward us. We cannot believe with certainty that we are pleasing to him. Besides, "our adversary, the devil, prowls around, issuing terrible roars" (1 Peter 5:8). He roars: "God is wrathful with you and will destroy you forever." We have nothing to strengthen and sustain us except the bare Word which sets Christ forth as the victor over sin, death, and every evil. But it is effort and labor to cling firmly to this in the midst of trial and conflict. We do not see Christ, and in the trial our heart does not feel his presence and help. Then we feel the power of sin, the weakness of the flesh, and our doubt. We feel the fiery darts of the devil (Eph. 6:16).

Meanwhile, the Holy Spirit is helping us in our weakness and interceding for us. He merely utters the words of a cry and a sigh, which is "Oh, Father!" This is indeed a very short word, but it includes everything. It is as if one were to say: "Even though I am surrounded by anxieties and seem to be deserted and banished from thy presence, nevertheless I am a child of God on account of Christ. I am beloved on account of the Beloved."

Therefore the term "Father," when spoken meaningfully in the heart, is an eloquence that Demosthenes, Cicero, and the most eloquent orators cannot attain.

Lectures on Galatians (1535)
LW 26, 380-81, 385

33

"And I will ask the Father, and he will give you another Advocate, to be with you forever."
—John 14:16

Here we must note in what a friendly and comforting manner Christ speaks to all poor, saddened hearts and fearful, timid consciences. He shows us how we may truly recognize the Holy Spirit. We must learn to know and believe in the Holy Spirit as Christ describes him. His is not a Spirit of anger and terror but a Spirit of grace and consolation. We are to know that the entire Deity reflects sheer comfort. The Father wants to comfort, for it is he who grants the Holy Spirit. The Son likewise, for he prays for this. And the Holy Spirit himself is to be the Comforter [Advocate]. Here, therefore, there is no wrath, threat, or terror for Christians; there is only a friendly smile and sweet comfort in heaven and on earth.

But we forget. The devil is too powerful among us, the world is too strong, and we see so many obstacles and temptations before us that we forget and cannot comprehend the comfort God sends into our hearts. We feel only that which hurts us. It is so strong that it fills one's whole being and erases these words from one's mind.

Therefore Christians should rise above all fear and sadness and hear Christ: "I know this very well, and for this very reason I am telling you about it in advance. You should not be guided by such feelings or believe your own thoughts; you should believe my word. For I will ask the Father and he will surely give you the Holy Spirit to comfort you. Then you can rest assured that I love you, the Father loves you, and the Holy Spirit, who is sent to you, loves you."

Sermons on the Gospel of St. John (1537)
LW 24, 103, 110-11, 114

34

When the Spirit of truth comes, he will guide you
into all the truth.
—John 16:13a

The Holy Spirit will teach the disciples and show them that everything Christ told them is the truth, for he is a Spirit who confirms the truth in one's heart and makes one sure of it.

The dear apostles surely found out, and their conduct toward their Lord Christ demonstrated adequately, how completely impossible—not only difficult—it is to retain faith in trials if one does not have the help of the Holy Spirit. In Christ's suffering and death they deserted him ignominiously. They denied him, and the faith in their hearts was practically extinguished by the thought inspired by the devil.

Thus true Christians always have discovered and still do that this faith, which should hold firmly to the articles concerning Christ and his kingdom, cannot be retained by human reason or power. The Holy Spirit himself must accomplish this. It is a sure sign of the presence of the Holy Spirit and of his power when faith is preserved and is victorious in a real battle and trial.

All experience and the work itself show daily that in Christendom the Holy Spirit himself must do everything that pertains to the real guidance of Christendom. For without him we would not baptize or preach very long nor would we retain the name of Christ. In one hour the devil would have dispossessed us of everything and would have destroyed it.

Sermons on the Gospel of St. John (1537)
LW 24, 357, 359-60

THE TRINITY

*"All that the Father has is mine. For this reason I said
that he will take what is mine and declare it to you."*
—John 16:15

THESE ARE ALL SUBLIME WORDS; FOR HERE CHRIST IS SPEAKING
in his own way, not about the creatures but about the sublime
and inscrutable essence in the Godhead.

Here the circle is completely closed, and all three—the
Father, the Son, and the Holy Spirit—are embraced in one
divine essence. Christ says: "From that which is mine, which is
the Father's, namely, the fact that I am one God with him, the
Holy Spirit also takes what he is and has. Therefore he is and has
exactly what both the Father and I are and have. For if he takes
and has what I have, it follows that he must be of the same nature
and essence, for what I have for myself and call my own cannot
be ascribed to any creature." Now "to take what is mine" does
not mean to take or cut off a fraction or a particle from the
Godhead, for the Godhead cannot be dismembered and
divided; it is a perfect, complete, and indivisible essence.
Accordingly, where there is a part, there the whole Godhead is
certainly present.

Sermons on the Gospel of St. John (1537)
LW 24, 372-73

And the Holy Spirit descended upon him in bodily form
like a dove. And a voice came from heaven, "You are my Son,
the Beloved; with you I am well pleased."
—Luke 3:22

The heavens opened, the Father's voice was heard, and the Holy Spirit descended, not as a phantom but in the form and figure of a natural dove. Nor was the Father's voice an illusion when he pronounced these words from heaven: "This is my beloved Son; with him I am well pleased." These were real, natural, human words. And this dove, in the form of which the Holy Spirit was seen, was real and natural. Nevertheless, it was the Holy Spirit.

All this was done in honor and praise of the Sacrament of Holy Baptism; for this is not a human institution but something sublime and holy. Eminent personages are involved in it: the Father who bestows and who speaks here; the Son, who receives and is baptized; the Holy Spirit, who hovers above and reveals himself in the form of a dove. And the celestial choir of all the angels is present; these skip and dance for joy over this act. Furthermore, the entire heaven stands ajar.

But it is recorded here that all three persons of the Trinity, God the Father, God the Son, and God the Holy Spirit, together with all the elect angels, were present at Christ's Baptism, although invisibly, and heaven was open for the occasion. In fact, God the Father, Son, and Holy Spirit still attend our Baptism today.

Sermons on the Gospel of St. John (1537-40)
LW 22, 173-74

[The Holy Spirit] will speak whatever he hears.
—John 16:13c

Here it is relevant to state that Scripture calls our Lord Christ—according to his divine nature—a "Word" (John 1:1), which the Father speaks with and in himself. Thus this word has a true, divine nature from the Father. It is not a word spoken by the Father as a physical, natural word spoken by a human being is a voice or a breath that does not remain within but comes out and remains outside. No, this word remains in the Father forever. Thus these are two distinct persons: he who speaks and the word that is spoken, that is, the Father and the Son.

Here, however, we find the third person following these two, namely, the one who hears both the speaker and the spoken word. For there must also be a listener where a speaker and a word are found. But all this speaking, being spoken, and listening takes place within the divine nature and also remains there, where no creature is or can be. All three—speaker, word, and listener—must be God himself. All three must be coeternal and in a single undivided majesty. For there is no difference or inequality in the divine essence, neither a beginning nor an end. Therefore, one cannot say that the listener is something outside God, or that there was a time when he began to be a listener. But just as the Father is a speaker from eternity, and just as the Son is spoken from eternity, so the Holy Spirit is the listener from eternity.

Sermons on the Gospel of St. John (1537)
LW 24, 364-65

*And God said, "Let the waters bring forth swarms
of living creatures . . ." So God created the great sea
monsters . . . And God saw that it was good.*
—Genesis 1:20-21

Here we must deal also with what the holy fathers, and Augustine in particular, have noted, namely, that Moses employs these three words—"God said," "He made [created]," "He saw"—as if in this manner he wanted to point to the three persons of the Divine Majesty. By the term "he said" the Father is denoted. He begets the Word in eternity and in time establishes this world through that Word. Therefore they have attributed the verb "made" to the person of the Son. The Son has in himself not only the image of the Divine Majesty but also the image of all created things. Therefore he bestows existence on things. Just as the objects are spoken by the Father, so all things have their existence through the Son and the word of the Father. To these, however, is joined the third person, the Holy Spirit, who "sees" the created things and approves them.

Further, according to St. Hilary, when the text says: "And God saw that it was very good," it refers to the preservation itself, because the creature could not continue in existence unless the Holy Spirit delighted in it and preserved the work through this delight of God in his work. God did not create things with the idea of abandoning them after they had been created, but he loves them and expresses his approval of them. Therefore he is together with them. He sets in motion, he moves, and he preserves each according to its own manner.

Lectures on Genesis (1535-36)
LW 1, 49-51

The king will desire your beauty.
Since he is your lord, bow to him.
—Psalm 45:11

I f we cannot grasp how God is one and three persons, we should leave that up to him. We should only incline our ear. He himself says that our king [Jesus Christ] is God, and he commands us to adore him. If you reject this king in the foolish superstition that you might break the First Commandment, then you have rejected the entire and true God, as the Arians [fourth century heretics] did.

If they object: "Then you make many gods," I reply: "I do not make another or many gods, but I say that Father, Son, and Holy Spirit are one and the same God. There is a unity of substance and one essence though there are three persons. I do not want to have many gods, because many gods contend among themselves. Nor can there be many gods. But here is unity. If I do not understand how the persons are differentiated, it is enough for me that Holy Scriptures say this and call Father, Son, and Holy Spirit by name (Matt. 28:19).

"If I could grasp this with my reason or senses, what need would there be for faith? Or what use is Scripture revealed by God through the Holy Spirit? If I believe nothing but what I can comprehend by my reason, I must reject Baptism, the Sacrament of the Altar, the Word, grace, original sin, and everything. Reason understands none of these things."

Commentary on "Psalm 45" (1532)
LW 12, 286-88

40

LAW AND GOSPEL

The law indeed was given through Moses; grace
and truth came through Jesus Christ.
—John 1:17

IT IS PROPER THAT THE LAW AND GOD'S COMMANDMENTS
provide me with the correct directives for life; they supply
me with abundant information about righteousness and eternal life. The Law is a sermon that points me to life, and it is
essential to remember this instruction. But it must be borne
in mind that the Law does not give me life. It resembles a
hand, which directs me to the right road. The hand gives me
the proper direction, but it will not conduct my steps along
the way.

Thus the Law serves to indicate the will of God, and it leads
us to a realization that we cannot keep it. It also acquaints us
with human nature, with its capabilities, and with its limita-
tions. The Law was given to us for the revelation of sin; but it
does not have the power to save us from sin and rid us of it. It
holds a mirror before us; we peer into it and perceive that we
are devoid of righteousness and life. And this image impels us to
cry: "Oh, come, Lord Jesus Christ, help us and give us grace to
enable us to fulfill the Law's demands!"

Sermons on the Gospel of St. John (1537-40)
LW 22, 143-44

*But now we are discharged from the law, dead to that
which held us captive, so that we are slaves not under
the old written code but in the new life of the Spirit.*
—Romans 7:6

But how are we "discharged from the Law"? Doubtless because through faith in Christ we satisfy the demands of the Law and through grace are freed and voluntarily perform the works of the Law. But those who do not have this faith are active in works unwillingly and almost in fear or in a desire for their own convenience. Therefore love is necessary, which seeks the things of God, love which is given to them who ask in faith and in the name of Jesus.

Even though we sin often and are not perfectly voluntary, yet we have made a beginning and are progressing, and we are righteous and free. But we must constantly beware that we not fall back under the Law. For who knows whether or not they are acting out of fear or a love for their own convenience even in a very subtle manner in their devotional life and their good works, looking for a rest and a reward rather than the will of God?

Therefore we must always remain in faith and pray for love.

Lectures on Romans (1515-16)
LW 25, 59-60

He said to them, "Go into all the world
and proclaim the good news to the whole creation."
——Mark 16:15

Gospel" [Euangelium] is a Greek word and means in Greek *a good message, good tidings, good news, a good report, which one sings and tells with gladness.* For example, when David overcame the great Goliath, there came among the Jewish people the good report and encouraging news that their terrible enemy had been struck down and that they had been rescued and given joy and peace. They sang and danced and were glad for it (1 Sam. 18:6).

Thus this gospel of God or New Testament is a good story and report, sounded forth into all the world by the apostles, telling of a true David who strove with sin, death, and the devil, and overcame them, and thereby rescued all those who were captive in sin, afflicted with death, and overpowered by the devil. Without any merit of their own he made them righteous, gave them life, and saved them, so that they were given peace and brought back to God. For this they sing, and thank and praise God, and are glad forever, if only they believe firmly and remain steadfast in faith.

"Prefaces to the New Testament" (1522, revised 1546)
LW 35, 358

43

He [Jesus] said to them, "Thus it is written, that the Messiah
is to suffer and to rise from the dead on the third day, and
that repentance and forgiveness of sins is to be proclaimed in
his name to all nations, beginning from Jerusalem."
—Luke 24:46-47

The gospel, then, is nothing but the preaching about Christ, Son of God and of David, true God and true human, who by his death and resurrection has overcome for us the sin, death, and hell of all who believe in him.

See to it, therefore, that you do not make a Moses out of Christ, or a book of laws and doctrines out of the gospel. For the gospel does not expressly demand works of our own by which we become righteous and are saved; indeed it condemns such works. Rather the gospel demands faith in Christ: that he has overcome for us sin, death, and hell, and thus gives us righteousness, life, and salvation not through our works, but through his own works, death, and suffering, in order that we may avail ourselves of his death and victory as though we had done it ourselves.

"Prefaces to the New Testament"(1522, revised 1546)
LW 35, 360

On the last day of the festival, the great day,
while Jesus was standing there, he cried out,
"Let anyone who is thirsty come to me."
—*John 7:37*

This is the thirst that is not appeased until Christ appears and says: "If you would like to be content and enjoy peace of mind and a good conscience, I advise you to come to me. Give up Moses and your works. Learn the difference between me and Moses. Your thirst you got from Moses. His role and his office were to frighten you and to make you thirsty. But now come to me, believe in me, hear my doctrine. I am a different type of preacher; I will give you drink and refresh you."

A person who masters the art of exact distinction between the Law and the Gospel should be called a real theologian. These two must be kept apart. The function of the Law is to frighten people and drive them to despair until they realize their inability to meet the demands of the Law or to obtain grace.

But Christ says: "Accept this from me. You lack piety, but I have kept the Law for you. Your sins are forgiven." Both the Law and the Gospel must be taught and considered. It is a mistake to confine yourself to one of the two. The Law serves no other purpose than to create a thirst and to frighten the heart. The Gospel alone satisfies the thirst, makes us cheerful, and revives and consoles the conscience. Lest the teaching of the Gospel create lazy, gluttonous Christians who think they need not perform good works, the Law tells the old Adam: "Refrain from sin! Be pious! Desist from this, and do that!" Then, when the conscience becomes depressed and realizes that the Law is not a mere cipher, one becomes frightened. And then one must give ear to the voice of the Gospel. When you have sinned, hearken to the teacher, Christ, who says: "Come to me! I will not let you die of thirst but will give you drink."

Sermons on the Gospel of St. John (1530-32)
LW 23, 271-72

45

CHRISTIAN RIGHTEOUSNESS

*For in [the gospel] the righteousness of God
is revealed through faith for faith; as it is written,
"The one who is righteous will live by faith."*
—Romans 1:17

HE IS NOT RIGHTEOUS WHO DOES MUCH, BUT HE WHO, WITHOUT work, believes much in Christ. For the righteousness of God is not acquired by means of acts frequently repeated, as Aristotle taught, but it is imparted by faith, for "The one who through faith is righteous shall live" (Rom. 1:17), and "One believes with the heart and so is justified" (Rom. 10:10). Therefore I wish to have the words "without work" understood in the following manner: Not that the righteous person does nothing, but that the works do not make the person righteous; rather that the righteousness creates works. For grace and faith are infused without our works. After they have been imparted the works follow.

Thus Romans 3:20 states, "No human being will be justified in his sight by works of the Law," and, "For we hold that a person is justified by faith apart from works of Law" (Rom. 3:28). In other words, works contribute nothing to justification. Therefore believers know that works that they do by such faith are not theirs but God's. For this reason they do not seek to become justified or glorified through them, but seek God. Their justification by faith in Christ is sufficient to them. Christ is their wisdom, righteousness, all things, as 1 Corinthians 1:30 has it, that they themselves may be Christ's vessels and instruments.

"Heidelberg Disputation"(1518)
LW 31, 55-56

"And when he comes, he will prove the world wrong
about sin and righteousness and judgment:
about righteousness, because I am going
to the Father and you will see me no longer."
—John 16:8, 10

These words show exhaustively that Christ is not speaking here of outward, secular righteousness, which is important and necessary for this life. He is speaking here of a righteousness recognized by God, a righteousness far different from that acknowledged by the world. This righteousness he exalts far above all the works that can be done in this life and identifies it exclusively with himself.

This is a peculiar righteousness. It is strange indeed that we are to be called righteous or to possess a righteousness, which is really no work, no thought, in short, nothing whatever in us but is entirely outside us in Christ. Yet it becomes truly ours by reason of his grace and gift, and becomes our very own, as though we ourselves had achieved and earned it.

47

Reason, of course, cannot comprehend this way of speaking, which says that our righteousness is something that involves nothing active or passive on our part. Yes, something in which I do not participate with my thoughts, perception, and senses; that nothing at all in me makes me pleasing to God and saves me; but that I leave myself and all human thoughts and ability out of account and cling to Christ, who sits up there at the right hand of God and whom I do not even see.

But in this verse I hear Christ say that my righteousness consists of his ascension into heaven. There my righteousness has been deposited, and there the devil will surely have to let it remain; for he will not make Christ a sinner or reprove or find fault with his righteousness.

Sermons on the Gospel of St. John (1537)
LW 24, 345-48

*For we hold that a person is justified by faith
apart from works prescribed by the law.*
—*Romans 3:28*

But the devil, that master of a thousand tricks, lays traps for us with marvelous cleverness. He leads some astray by getting them involved in open sins. Others, who think themselves righteous, he brings to a stop, makes them lukewarm as Revelation 3:14ff. A third group he seduces into superstitions and ascetic sects, so that, for example, they do not at all grow cold but feverishly engage in works, setting themselves apart from the others, whom they despise in their pride and disdain. A fourth class of people he urges on with ridiculous labor to the point where they try to be completely pure and holy, without any taint of sin.

He senses the weakness of each individual and attacks him in this area. And because these four classes of people are so fervent for righteousness, it is not easy to persuade them to the contrary. Thus he begins by helping them to achieve their goal, so that they become overanxious to rid themselves of every evil desire. When they cannot accomplish this, he causes them to become sad, dejected, wavering, hopeless, and unsettled in their consciences.

Then it only remains for us to stay in our sins and to cry in hope of the mercy of God that he would deliver us from them. Just as the patient who is too anxious to recover can surely have a serious relapse, we must also be healed gradually and for a while put up with certain weaknesses. For it is sufficient that our sin displeases us, even though we do not get entirely rid of it. For Christ carries all sins, if only they are displeasing to us, and thus they are no longer ours but his, and his righteousness in turn is ours.

Lectures on Romans (1515-16)
LW 25, 254

*I have been crucified with Christ; and it is no longer
I who live, but it is Christ who lives in me.*
—Galatians 2:19b-20a

Paul shows how he is alive, and he states what Christian righteousness is. It is that righteousness by which Christ lives in us. Christ and my conscience must become one, so that nothing remains in my sight but Christ, crucified and risen. If I look only at myself, then I am done for. By paying attention to myself and considering what my condition is or should be, and what I am supposed to be doing, I lose sight of Christ.

This is an extremely common evil. In such conflicts of conscience, therefore, we must form the habit of leaving ourselves behind as well as the Law and all our works, which force us to pay attention to ourselves. We must turn our eyes completely to that bronze serpent, Christ nailed to the cross (John 3:14). We must declare with assurance that he is our righteousness and life. For the Christ on whom our gaze is fixed, in whom we exist, and who also lives in us, is the victor and the Lord over the Law, sin, death, and every evil. In him a sure comfort has been set forth for us, and victory has been granted.

49

Therefore, because Christ clings and dwells in us most intimately, we can say: "Christ is fixed and cemented to me and abides in me. The life that I now live, he lives in me. Indeed, Christ himself is the life that I now live."

Lectures on Galatians (1535)
LW 26, 166-67

*Out of his anguish he shall see light; he shall find
satisfaction through his knowledge. The righteous one,
my servant, shall make many righteous,
and he shall bear their iniquities.*
—Isaiah 53:11

A Christian cannot arrive at this knowledge by means of any laws, either moral or civil, but he must ascend to heaven by means of the Gospel. This is the vehicle by which the knowledge of God reaches us. There is no other plan or method of obtaining liberty than the knowledge of Christ. You must therefore note this new definition of righteousness. Righteousness is the knowledge of Christ, the one who bears all our sins.

The individual words his knowledge and iniquities must be pondered in supreme faith. They must be read and considered with the most watchful eyes, so that it is not simply any kind of knowledge or understanding but a knowledge that justifies. Thus you see this remarkable definition of righteousness through the knowledge of God. It sounds ridiculous to call righteousness a speculative knowledge. Therefore it is said in Jer. 9:24: "Let him who glories glory in this, that he understands and knows me."

This knowledge, then, is the formal and substantial righteousness of the Christians, that is, faith in Christ, which I obtain through the Word. I receive the Word through the intellect, but to assent to that Word is the work of the Holy Spirit. It is not the work of reason, which always seeks its own kinds of righteousness. The Word, however, sets forth another righteousness through the consideration and the promises of Scripture, which cause this faith to be accounted for righteousness. This is our glory to know for certain that our righteousness is divine in that God does not impute our sins. Therefore our righteousness is nothing else than knowing God.

Lectures on Isaiah (1527-30)
LW 17, 229-30

50

FAITH ALONE

Yet we know that a person is justified not by the works
of the law but through faith in Jesus Christ.
—Galatians 2:16a

CHRISTIAN FAITH IS NOT AN IDLE QUALITY OR AN EMPTY HUSK in the heart, which may exist in a state of mortal sin until love comes along to make it alive. But if it is true faith, it is a sure trust and firm acceptance in the heart. It takes hold of Christ in such a way that Christ is the object of faith, or rather not the object but, so to speak, the one who is present in the faith itself.

Thus faith is a sort of knowledge or darkness that nothing can see. Yet the Christ of whom faith takes hold is sitting in the darkness as God sat in the midst of darkness on Sinai and in the temple. Therefore our "formal righteousness" is not a love that informs faith; but it is faith itself, a cloud in our hearts, that is, trust in a thing we do not see, in Christ, who is present especially when he cannot be seen. Therefore faith justifies because it takes hold of and possesses this treasure, the present Christ.

Lectures on Galatians (1535)
LW 26, 129-30

So you are no longer a slave but a child,
and if a child then also an heir, through God.
—Galatians 4:7

It transcends all the capacity of the human mind when he says "heirs," not of some very wealthy and powerful king, but of Almighty God, the Creator of all. If someone could believe with a certain and constant faith, he could regard all the power and wealth of all the world as filth in comparison with his heavenly inheritance. For what is the whole world in comparison to heaven?

He would desire to depart and to be with Christ. Nothing more delightful could happen to him than a premature death, for he would know that it is the end of all his evils and that through it he comes into his inheritance. A person who believed this completely would not go on living very long. He would soon be consumed by his overwhelming joy.

But the law in our members at war with the law of our mind (Rom. 7:23) does not permit faith to be perfect. We need the aid and comfort of the Holy Spirit. Paul himself exclaims (Rom. 7:24): "Wretched man that I am! Who will deliver me from this body of death?" He did not always have pleasant and happy thoughts about his future inheritance in heaven. Over and over he experienced sadness of spirit and fear.

From this it is evident how difficult a thing faith is. For a perfect faith would soon bring a perfect contempt and scorn for this present life. We would not attach our hearts so firmly to physical things that their presence would give us confidence and their removal would produce dejection and even despair. But we would do everything with complete love, humility, and patience.

Lectures on Galatians (1535)
LW 26, 392-93

*For in Christ Jesus neither circumcision nor
uncircumcision counts for anything; the only thing
that counts is faith working through love.*
—Galatians 5:6

Here Paul presents the Christian life—faith that is neither imaginary nor hypocritical but true and living. It is a faith that arouses and motivates good works through love. He says: "It is true that faith alone justifies, without works. But I am speaking about genuine faith. After it has justified, it will not go to sleep but it is active through love."

Thus he describes the whole Christian life. Inwardly it is faith toward God, and outwardly it is love or works toward one's neighbor. In this way a person is a Christian in a total sense. Inwardly through faith in the sight of God, who does not need our works; outwardly in the sight of other people, who do not derive any benefit from our faith but do derive benefit from works or from our love.

53

Earlier Paul has discussed the internal nature of faith and has taught that it is righteousness or rather justification in the sight of God. Here he connects it with love and works; that is, he speaks of its external function. He says that it is the impulse and motivation of good works or of love toward one's neighbor. Thus it is true faith toward God, which loves and helps one's neighbor. This is the total life of Christians.

Lectures on Galatians (1535)
LW 27, 28, 30-31

Therefore, since we are justified by faith, we have peace
with God through our Lord Jesus Christ, through whom we
have obtained access to this grace in which we stand;
and we boast in our hope of sharing the glory of God.
—Romans 5:1, 2

God in his grace has provided us with a man in whom we may trust, rather than in our works. He wants us to rely on Christ so that we will not waver in ourselves nor be satisfied with the righteousness, which has begun in us unless it cleaves to and flows from Christ's righteousness, and so that no fool, having once accepted the gift, will think himself already contented and secure. But he does not want us to halt in what has been received, but rather to draw near from day to day so that we may be fully transformed into Christ.

His righteousness is perpetual and sure; there is no change, there is there no lack, for he himself is the Lord of all. Therefore whenever Paul preached faith in Christ, he did so with the utmost care to proclaim that righteousness is not only through him or from him, but even that it is in him. He draws us into himself, and transforms us, and places us as if in hiding "until the wrath passes away" (Isa. 26:20). Observe, faith is not enough, but only the faith that hides under the wings of Christ and glories in his righteousness.

Paul teaches faith in such a way as to thrust it under the wings of Christ. Faith is precisely that which makes you a chick, and Christ a hen, so that you have hope under his wings. To have faith is to cleave to him, to presume on him, because he is holy and just for you.

"Against Latomus"(1521)
LW 32, 235-36

The only thing that counts is faith working through love.
—Galatians 5:6b

St. Paul does not speak here about what faith is or does by its own work (which he abundantly teaches earlier throughout the whole epistle), nor does he speak about what love is or does; rather, he briefly summarizes what an entire Christian life should be, namely, faith and love; faith in God, which apprehends Christ and receives forgiveness of sins apart from all works, and after that love toward the neighbor, which as the fruit of faith proves that faith is true and not lazy or false, but active and living. For that reason he does not say that love is active but, rather, that faith is active, that faith practices love and makes it active. St. Paul ascribes everything to faith, which not only receives grace from God but also is active toward the neighbor and out of itself gives birth to and produces love or works.

Treatise on "The Private Mass and the Consecration of Priests" (1533)
LW 38, 184

GRACE

There is therefore now no condemnation
for those who are in Christ Jesus.
—Romans 8:1

BETWEEN GRACE AND GIFT THERE IS THIS DIFFERENCE. GRACE
actually means God's favor, or the good will which in himself he
bears toward us, by which he is disposed to give us Christ and to
pour into us the Holy Spirit with his gifts. The gifts and the
Spirit increase in us every day, but they are not yet perfect for
there remain in us the evil desires and sins that war against the
Spirit. Nevertheless grace does so much that we are accounted
completely righteous before God. For his grace is not divided or
parceled out, as are the gifts, but takes us completely into favor
for the sake of Christ our Intercessor and Mediator. And because
of this, the gifts are begun in us.

"Preface to the Epistle of St. Paul to the Romans"(1522, revised 1546)
LW 35, 369-70

For your name's sake, O LORD, preserve my life.
In your righteousness bring me out of trouble . . .
for I am your servant.
—Psalm 143:11-12

I live in grace. Therefore my whole life serves thee, not myself, for I seek not myself but thee and thine. Those who live in their own righteousness cannot do this. They serve themselves and look for their own welfare in all things.

Now someone might say to me: "Can't you ever do anything but speak only about the righteousness, wisdom, strength of God rather than of humanity, always expounding Scripture from the standpoint of God's righteousness and grace, always harping on the same string and singing the same old song?"

I answer: Let each one look to himself. As for me, I confess: Whenever I found less in the Scriptures than Christ, I was never satisfied; but whenever I found more than Christ, I never became poorer. Therefore it seems to me to be true that God the Holy Spirit does not know and does not want to know anything besides Jesus Christ, as he says of him (John 16:13-14): "He will glorify Me; he will not speak of himself, but he will take of mine and declare it to you."

57

Christ is God's grace, mercy, righteousness, truth, wisdom, power, comfort, and salvation, given to us by God without any merit on our part. Christ, I say, not as some express it in blind words, "causally," that he grants righteousness and remains absent himself, for that would be dead. Yes, it is not given at all unless Christ himself is present, just as the radiance of the sun and the heat of fire are not present if there is no sun and no fire.

Commentary on "The Seven Penitential Psalms" (1525)
LW 14, 204

He will not cry or lift up his voice,
or make it heard in the street.
—Isaiah 42:2

he prophet says that Christ himself will not be noisy in the streets nor make himself heard in the open. How does this jibe? The noise is of two kinds: the noise of wrath and that of love. He did indeed cry in the preaching proceeding from love, but not in a noisy way, as the self-righteous and other sects are noisy. In opposition to their harshest clamor the prophet depicts the office of Christ as being most gentle and mild. This is to cry without being noisy, that is, teach gently without rage.

In other partisan groups and judgments and lawsuits there is nothing but accusation and shouting on the part of those who suffer wrong on both sides. Even judges shout when they pass sentence. Thus the self-righteous are most turbulent. Because all of them are by nature sad and stern, all of them are ready to pass judgment. They measure everything by the standard of their own life and most severely condemn everything else.

True righteousness, however, has compassion, while the false has condemnation. Here in Christ you see the gentlest and most agreeable appearance. This is what it means for Christians not to raise their voices, that is, in an uproar, but rather in grace.

Lectures on Isaiah (1527-30)
LW 17, 64

58

And why not say (as some people slander us by saying that
we say),"Let us do evil so that good may come"?
—Romans 3:8

The apostle is not speaking primarily against those who are open sinners. He is speaking against those who appear righteous in their own eyes and trust in their own works for salvation. He is trying to encourage these people to magnify the grace of God, which cannot be magnified unless sin, which is forgiven through this grace, is first acknowledged and magnified.

This is why the others, when they heard this, were offended and thought that the apostle is preaching that evil should be done, so that the glory of God might be magnified. For in this way do our iniquity and our lying "Abound to his glory" (v. 7), when we, humbled through the confession of them, glorify God, who has forgiven such wickedness out of his overflowing grace. He would not be glorified in this way if we did not believe that we are in need of his grace but thought that we were sufficient of ourselves in his sight. Thus those are better off who acknowledge that they have many sins and no righteousness than those who like a Pharisee acknowledge that they have much righteousness and no sin. For the one glorifies the mercy of God, but the other their own righteousness.

Lectures on Romans (1515-16)
LW 25, 28

59

[The Son of God] loved me and gave himself for me.
—Galatians 2:20b

Read these words "me" and "for me" with great emphasis. Accustom yourself to accepting this "me" with a sure faith and applying it to yourself. Do not doubt that you belong to the number of those who speak this "me."

It is as though Paul were saying: "The Law did not love me. It did not give itself for me. It accuses and frightens me. Now I have another, who has freed me from the terrors of the Law, from sin, and from death. He is One who has transferred me into freedom, the righteousness of God, and eternal life. He is called the Son of God."

Therefore Christ is not Moses, not a taskmaster or a law-giver. He is the Dispenser of grace, the Savior, and the Pitier. In other words, he is nothing but sheer, infinite mercy, which gives and is given.

For Christ is the joy and sweetness to a trembling and troubled heart. He is the One "who loved me and gave himself for me."

Christ did not love only Peter and Paul, but the same grace belongs and comes to us. We are included in this "me." For just as we cannot deny that we are sinners, so we cannot deny that Christ died for our sins.

Lectures on Galatians (1535)
LW 26, 177-79

FORGIVENESS

The next day [John] saw Jesus coming toward him
and declared, "Here is the Lamb of God who takes
away the sin of the world!"
—John 1:29

ANYONE WHO WISHES TO BE SAVED MUST KNOW THAT ALL HIS
sins have been placed on the back of this lamb! Therefore John
points this lamb out to his disciples, saying: "Do you want to
know where the sins of the world are placed for forgiveness?
Then don't resort to the Law of Moses or betake yourselves to
the devil. There, to be sure, you will find sins, but sins to terrify
you and damn you. But if you really want to find a place where
the sins of the world are exterminated and deleted, then cast
your gaze upon the cross. The Lord places all our sins on the
back of this lamb. . . ."

Therefore a Christian must cling simply to this verse and let
no one rob him of it. For there is no other comfort either in
heaven or on earth to fortify us against all attacks and temptations, especially in the agony of death.

Christ does bear the sin—not only mine and yours or that
of any other individual, or only of one kingdom or country, but
the sin of the entire world. And you, too, are a part of the world.

Sermon on the Gospel of St. John (1537-40)
LW 22, 163-64

For what the flesh desires is opposed to the Spirit, and what the Spirit desires is opposed to the flesh; for these are opposed to each other, to prevent you from doing what you want.
—Galatians 5:17

I remember that Staupitz [Luther's friend and one-time superior] used to say: "More than a thousand times I have vowed to God that I would improve, but I have never performed what I have vowed. Hereafter I shall not make such vows, because I know perfectly well that I shall not live up to them. Unless God is gracious and merciful to me for the sake of Christ and grants me a blessed final hour, I shall not be able to stand before him with all my vows and good works." This despair is not only truthful but is godly and holy. Whoever wants to be saved must make this confession with the mouth and with the heart.

The saints do not rely on their own righteousness. They gaze at Christ, their propitiator. If there is any remnant of sin in the flesh, they know that this is not imputed to them but is pardoned. Meanwhile they battle by the Spirit against the flesh. This does not mean that they do not feel its desires at all; it means that they do not gratify them. Even though they feel the flesh raging and rebelling in them, they do not become downcast. No, they fortify themselves with their faith.

Therefore let none despair when they feel their flesh begin another battle against the Spirit, or if they do not succeed immediately in forcing their flesh to be subject to the Spirit. But let them be aroused and incited to seek forgiveness of sins through Christ and to embrace the righteousness of faith.

Lectures on Galatians (1535)
LW 27, 72-74

Guard the doors of your mouth from her
who lies in your embrace.
—Micah 7:5b

Here the prophet does not want suspicion and hatred to exist between spouses. He wants the utmost love and good will, which cannot exist without mutual trust. And yet he wants a limit to this trust, because it can happen that it is mistaken. For your spouse is a human being. Although this spouse fears God and pays heed to his word, nevertheless, because Satan, the enemy, is lying in wait everywhere and because human nature is weak, your spouse can fall and disappoint your hope somewhere.

When you foresee this with your mind, you will be more ready to forgive, and you will be less distressed if anything happens contrary to what you had hoped. Thus love will remain, and harmony will not be disturbed. For nothing has happened that was not anticipated, and love is readiest to forgive. This is indeed a rare gift, but because you are a Christian, remember that this ought to be your attitude.

And so with others, Christians hate no one, and yet they trust no one. If others show them some kindness, they consider this an advantage and delight in it, nevertheless in such a way that if the kindness should cease or some adversity should occur, they would not be provoked or begin to hate the other person. For those who are taught by the Holy Scriptures realize what is in humanity, and for this reason they place complete trust in God and not in humans; yet they love all equally and show kindness to all, even to their enemies.

This, then, is solid friendship and the most steadfast love. It has its source, not in our judgment but in the Holy Spirit, who urges our minds to follow the Word.

Lectures on Genesis (ca. 1536)
LW 2, 299-302

If we confess our sins, he who is faithful and just and will
forgive us our sins and cleanse us from all unrighteousness.
—1 John 1:9

I n this Christian Church, wherever it exists, is to be found the forgiveness of sins, that is, a kingdom of grace and of true pardon. For in it are found the gospel, baptism, and the sacrament of the altar, in which the forgiveness of sins is offered, obtained, and received. But this forgiveness of sins is not to be expected only at one time, as in baptism, but frequently, as often as one needs it, till death.

For this reason I have a high regard for private confession, for here God's word and absolution are spoken privately and individually to each believer for the forgiveness of sins, and as often as believers desire it they may have recourse to it for this forgiveness, and also for comfort, counsel, and guidance. Thus it is a precious, useful thing for souls, as long as no one is driven to it with laws and commandments. But sinners are to be left free to make use of it, according to their own needs, when and where they wish; just as we are free to obtain counsel and comfort, guidance and instruction when and where our need or our inclination moves us. Private confession is worthwhile as long as one is not forced to enumerate all sins but only those which oppress one most grievously, or those which a person will mention.

"Confession Concerning Christ's Supper"(1528)
LW 37, 368

*You were running well; who prevented you
from obeying the truth? Such persuasion
does not come from the one who calls you.*
—*Galatians 5:7-8*

T his comfort applies to all who, in their affliction and temptation, develop a false idea of Christ. For Satan has a thousand tricks and turns the comfort of Christ upside down by setting against it the example of Christ. He says: "But your life does not correspond to Christ's either in word or in deed. You have done nothing good." When this happens, one who has been assailed should be comforted this way: "Scripture presents Christ in two ways. First as a gift. If I take hold of him this way, I shall lack nothing whatever. As great as he is, he has been made by God my wisdom, righteousness, sanctification, and redemption (1 Cor. 1:30). Even if I have committed many great sins, nevertheless, if I believe in him, they are swallowed up by his righteousness.

"Secondly, Scripture presents him as an example for us to imitate. But I will not let this Christ be presented to me as exemplar except at a time of rejoicing, when I am out of reach of temptations, so that I may have a mirror in which to contemplate how much I am still lacking, lest I become smug. But in a time of tribulation I will only see and hear Christ as a gift, as him who died for my sins, who has bestowed his righteousness on me, and who accomplished and fulfilled what is lacking in my life."

Lectures on Galatians (1535)
LW 27, 33-34

Christ in Us

[I pray] that Christ may dwell
in your hearts through faith.
—Ephesians 3:17a

HOW THEN DO WE HAVE CHRIST? AH, YOU CANNOT HAVE HIM except in the gospel in which he is promised to you. And because Christ comes into our heart through the gospel, he must also be accepted by the heart. As I now believe that he is in the gospel, so I receive him and have him already. So Paul says: I carry Christ in my heart, for he is mine (cf. Eph. 3:17).

When we have Christ by true faith, then he causes us to live in such a way that we are strengthened in faith, in such a way that I do these works that I do for the benefit and good of my neighbor. For my Christian name would not be sufficient, despite my baptism and my faith, if I did not help my neighbors and draw them to faith through my works in order that they may follow me. Then believers, after they have given all glory to Christ, are always remembering to do to their neighbor as Christ has done to them, in order that they may help the neighbor and everyone else. Thus Christ lives in them and they live for the betterment of their neighbor, giving to everyone a good example of doing all things in love.

"Two Sermons Preached at Weimar" (The Second) (1522)
LW 51, 114, 116

I have been crucified with Christ; and it is no longer
I who live, but it is Christ who lives in me.
—*Galatians 2:19b-20a*

Who is this "I" of whom Paul says: "Yet not I"? It is the one that has the Law and is obliged to do works, the one that is a person separate from Christ. This "I" Paul rejects; for "I" as a person distinct from Christ, belongs to death and hell. That is why he says: "Not I, but Christ lives in me." Christ is my "form," which adorns my faith as color or light adorns a wall. "Christ," he says, "is fixed and cemented to me and abides in me. The life that I now live, he lives in me. Indeed, Christ himself is the life that I now live. In this way, therefore, Christ and I are one."

Living in me as he does, Christ abolishes the Law, damns sin, and kills death; for at his presence all these cannot help disappearing. Christ is eternal peace, comfort, righteousness, and life, to which the terror of the Law, sadness of mind, sin, hell, and death have to yield. Abiding and living in me, Christ removes and absorbs all the evils that torment and afflict me. This attachment to him causes me to be liberated from the terror of the Law and of sin, pulled out of my own skin, and transferred into Christ and into his kingdom, which is a kingdom of grace, righteousness, peace, joy, life, salvation, and eternal glory. Because I am in him, no evil can harm me.

67

Lectures on Galatians (1535)
LW 26, 167

Light rises in the darkness for the upright;
the Lord is gracious, merciful, and righteous.
—Psalm 112:4 (Luther's translation)

Light, joy, and pleasure, all things, are received by upright believers from him who is gracious, merciful, and righteous toward them. It is based on their conviction that their hearts are right with him who is good, gracious, and merciful. Then they have no misgivings, but are confident.

The hypocrites and the wicked also call God gracious, merciful, and righteous. But they do not understand it. They read and sing and preach about it, but there is a big difference. It is one thing to preach, sing, and say that God is all these things. It is quite another to feel the gracious, merciful, and righteous God in the heart. The pious and upright have this not only on their tongue but also in their heart. When the tongue and the heart agree, then it is well. But if this lies in the mouth alone, and the heart is a hundred thousand miles away, then it is futile. Christians feel and experience it in their heart that those matters do not happen accidentally or come from mortals. They feel it in their heart, are sure about it, and do not doubt.

Now, they who feel this in their heart will be satisfied. The light rises for them in the darkness. When the darkness is past, they also become rich and rise high, even if they are poor and oppressed. For they have him who is gracious and merciful. Now, if they have him who is the fountain and source of all things, what could they lack?

Commentary on "Psalm 112" (1526)
LW 13, 391, 405

"If you abide in me, and my words abide in you . . ."
—John 15:7a

Note how highly this man extols the Christian life. In case someone has not understood and would like to ask: "But how, my dear man, does one remain in Christ? How am I a branch in this vine, or how do I remain a branch?"

Christ answers: "Just pay attention to my word. Everything depends on whether my word remains in you, that is whether you believe and confess the article taught in the children's (Apostles') Creed: 'I believe in Jesus Christ, our Lord, who was crucified for me, who died, rose again, and is seated at the right hand of the Father,' and whatever pertains to it. If you remain faithful to this and are ready to stake all on it, to forsake all rather than accept a different doctrine or works, if you thus remain in the Word, then I remain in you and you in me. Then our roots are intertwined; then we are joined, so that my words and your heart have become one. Then you will not ask further how I abide in you or you in me, for you will see this in yonder life. Now, however, you can grasp and comprehend it in no other way than that you have my word, that you are washed in my blood by faith, and that you are anointed and sealed with my spirit. Therefore your whole life and all your deeds are acceptable and nothing but good fruit."

69

Sermons on the Gospel of St. John (1537)
LW 24, 238-39

First, I thank my God through Jesus Christ for all of you,
because your faith is proclaimed throughout the world.
—Romans 1:8

his is the Christian and true way of praising people—not to praise people for their own sake but to praise God in them first and foremost and to attribute everything to him, as Isaiah 43:21 says: "This people have I formed for myself, they shall show forth my praise."

Then the apostle shows that God is not praised except through Christ. As we receive everything from God through him so we must return everything to God through him for he alone is worthy to appear before the face of God and to carry on his priestly office for us, as in Hebrews 13:15: "Through him then let us continually offer up a sacrifice of praise to God, that is, the fruits of lips that acknowledge his name."

Therefore, he praises God through Christ for these people. While it is characteristic of envy to be sad about a neighbor's good gifts and to curse them, here we see love. For it is the nature of love that it rejoices in the good gifts of the neighbor, especially his spiritual gifts, and glorifies God in them.

Lectures on Romans (1515-16)
LW 25, 6-7

CHRISTIAN FREEDOM

For though I am free with respect to all, I have made
myself a slave to all, so that I might win more of them.
—*1 Corinthians 9:19*

TO MAKE THE WAY SMOOTHER FOR THE UNLEARNED—FOR ONLY them do I serve—I shall set down the following two propositions concerning the freedom and the bondage of the spirit:

A Christian is a perfectly free lord of all, subject to none. A Christian is a perfectly dutiful servant of all, subject to all.

These two theses seem to contradict each other. If, however, they should be found to fit together they would serve our purpose beautifully. Both are Paul's own statements, who says in 1 Cor. 9:19, "For though I am free from all . . . I have made myself a slave to all," and in Rom. 13:8, "Owe no one anything, except to love one another." Love by its very nature is ready to serve and be subject to the one who is loved. So Christ, although he was Lord of all, was "born of woman, born under the law" (Gal. 4:4), and therefore was at the same time free and a servant, "in the form of God" and "of a servant" (Phil. 2:6-7).

So a Christian, like Christ his head, is filled and made rich by faith and should be content with this form of God, which he has obtained by faith. This faith is his life, his righteousness, and his salvation: it saves him and makes him acceptable, and bestows upon him all things that are Christ's. Although Christians are thus free from all works, they ought in this liberty to empty themselves, take upon themselves the form of a servant, be made in human likeness, be found in human form, and to serve, help, and in every way deal with their neighbor as they see that God through Christ has dealt and still deals with them.

Treatise on "The Freedom of a Christian" (1520)
LW 31, 344, 366

Jesus answered them, "Very truly, I tell you,
everyone who commits sin is a slave to sin."
—John 8:34

C hrist does not plan to alter secular kingdoms or to abolish serfdom. What does he care how princes and lords rule? It does not concern him how a person plows, sows, makes shoes, builds houses, or pays tribute or taxes. Such work was ordered in Gen. 1:28, when God created the world and specified that we should beget children and occupy and cultivate the world. Here Christ is not speaking about these external matters; rather he is speaking of a freedom that lies outside and above this outward existence and life. Here he deals with freedom from sin, death, God's wrath, the devil, hell, and eternal damnation.

This Christian freedom may be enjoyed both by one who is free and by one who is a bondservant, by one who is a captive and by one who takes others captive, by a woman as well as by a man, by a servant and a maid as well as by a lord and a lady. We are speaking of the freedom before God, the freedom we have when God pronounces us free from sin. This freedom is extended to all.

Sermons on the Gospel of St. John (1530-32)
LW 23, 404

For freedom Christ has set us free. Stand firm, therefore.
—Galatians 5:1a

Christ has set us free, not from some human slavery or tyrannical authority but from the eternal wrath of God. Where? In the conscience. This is where our freedom comes to a halt; it goes no further. For Christ has set us free, not for a political freedom or a freedom of the flesh but for a theological or spiritual freedom. Our conscience is free and joyful, unafraid of the wrath to come (Matt. 3:7). This is the most genuine freedom; it is immeasurable. For who can express what a great gift it is for someone to be able to declare for certain that God neither is nor ever will be wrathful but will forever be a gracious and merciful Father for the sake of Christ?

It is a great and incomprehensible freedom that is easier to talk about than it is to believe. If this freedom Christ has achieved for us could be grasped in its certainty, no fury or terror of the world, the Law, sin, death, the devil, could be too great. For it would swallow them up as quickly as the ocean swallows a spark. This freedom of Christ certainly swallows up and abolishes a whole heap of evils, and in their place it establishes righteousness, peace, life, and more. Blessed is the one who understands and believes this.

Lectures on Galatians (1535)
LW 27, 4-5

They are like trees planted by streams of water,
which yield their fruit in its season.
——Psalm 1:3a

To bring forth fruit indicates that these blessed ones, through love, serve not themselves but their neighbors. They are compared to a tree, which bears fruit not for itself, but for others. In fact, no creatures live for themselves or serve only themselves except human beings and the devil. The sun does not shine for itself, water does not flow for itself. Certainly every creature serves the law of love, and its whole substance is in the Law of the Lord. Even the members of the human body do not serve only themselves. Only the passions of the heart are ungodly. For this ungodly passion not only gives none their own, serves no one, is kind to no one, but snatches everything for itself, looks for its own in everything, even in God himself. But these blessed ones possess the kindness of the good trees, which do no one evil but help everyone, while willingly giving their fruits.

The blessed ones give these fruits "in their season." Oh, this is a golden lovable word, through which the freedom of the righteous Christian is affirmed! The ungodly have fixed days, fixed times, certain works, and certain places to which they are so firmly bound that even if their neighbor were to die of starvation, they could not tear themselves away to help. But the blessed ones are free at all times, in every work, for every place, and toward every person. Whatever the situation, they will serve you; and whatever their hands find to do, they will do it. They give their fruit in its season, as often as God or other people need their works.

"Psalm 1"(1519)
LW 14, 300-1

And the life I now live in the flesh I live by faith
in the Son of God, who loved me and gave himself for me.
—Galatians 2:20b

H e ought to think: "Although I am unworthy and condemned, my God has given me in Christ all the riches of righteousness and salvation without any merit on my part, out of pure, free mercy, so that from now on I need nothing except faith, which believes that this is true. Why should I not therefore freely, joyfully, with all my heart, and with an eager will do all things that I know are pleasing and acceptable to such a Father who has overwhelmed me with his inestimable riches? I will therefore give myself as a Christ to my neighbor, just as Christ offered himself to me. I will do nothing in this life except what I see is necessary, profitable, and salutary to my neighbor, because through faith I have an abundance of all good things in Christ."

Behold, from faith thus flow forth love and joy in the Lord, and from love a joyful, willing, and free mind that serves one's neighbor willingly and takes no account of gratitude or ingratitude, of praise or blame, of gain or loss. For believers do not serve that they may put others under obligations. They do not distinguish between friends and enemies or anticipate their thankfulness or unthankfulness, but they most freely and most willingly spend themselves and all that they have, whether they waste all on the thankless or whether they gain a reward.

Therefore, if we recognize the great and precious things that are given us, our hearts will be filled by the Holy Spirit and the love that makes us free, joyful, almighty workers and conquerors over all tribulations, servants of our neighbors, and yet lords of all.

Treatise on "The Freedom of a Christian" (1520)
LW 31, 367

HEARING GOD

But their delight is in the law of the LORD,
and on his law they meditate day and night.
—Psalm 1:2

THIS DELIGHT OR DESIRE COMES FROM FAITH IN GOD THROUGH Jesus Christ. On the other hand, a desire that has been extorted through fear of punishment is servile and impetuous, while that which is induced through a desire for reward is mercenary and false. But this person's desire is free; it does not seek reward and is happy. It becomes clear then that if this psalm is not understood of Christ alone, it becomes a mirror and a goal toward which the blessed person must strive.

But through this desire the believer has become one with the word of God as love unites the lover with the beloved. And the desire is the whole life of that person for wherever love goes, there the heart and the body follow. Here we are able to see the contrasting life of the pious and the impious. The ungodly begin their righteousness from the outside and proceed inward. First they pretend works, then words, and only afterwards do they practice thinking. This is the greatest height they reach.

The godly, on the other hand, begin from the inside. They start with this holy desire, and then follow meditation and external works, and after this the teaching of others. For it is the mode of nature of all who love to chatter, sing, think, compose, and frolic freely about what they love and to enjoy hearing about it. Therefore this lover, this blessed person, has this love, the Law of God, always in the mouth, always in the heart and, if possible, always in the ear. "Whoever is of God hears the words of God" (John 8:47).

"Psalm 1" (1519-21)
LW 14, 295, 297-98

And when he had finished talking with him,
God went up from Abraham.
—Genesis 17:22

t is indeed something very great to have God conversing and associating with us. Even though God does not appear to us in an extraordinary form as he did to Abraham, yet his usual and most friendly and most intimate appearance is this, that he presents himself to us in the Word, in Baptism, in the Lord's Supper, and in the use of the Keys [God's spiritual power given to the Christian Church to distribute the blessings of the Gospel (Matt. 18:18)].

These facts must be impressed rather frequently, and it is not without reason that I am repeating them. If Abraham should be compared with us who live in the New Testament, he is, for the most part, less important than we are, provided that one considers the matter impartially. To be sure, in his case the personal gifts are greater; but God did not manifest himself to him in a closer and more friendly manner than he does to us. Let it indeed be a great glory to have those appearances, but what greater or better advantage did Abraham have from them than the fact that God spoke with him?

This happens to us, too, and indeed daily, as often as and where ever we wish. It is true that you hear a human being when you are baptized and when you partake of the Holy Supper. But the Word that you hear is not that of a human being; it is the Word of the living God. It is he who baptizes you. It is he who absolves you from sins. It is he who commands you to hope in his mercy.

Lectures on Genesis (1538)
LW 3, 165-66

Anyone who resolves to do the will of God will know
whether the teaching is from God.
—John 7:17a

ow this is the will of the Father, that we be intent on hearing what the man Christ has to say, that we listen to his word. You must not quibble at his word, find fault with it, and dispute it. Just hear it.

Then the Holy Spirit will come and prepare your heart, that you may sincerely believe the preaching of the divine word, even give up your life for it, and say: "This is God's word and the pure truth." But if you insist that you be heard, that your reason interpret Christ's word; if you presume to play the master of the word, to propound other doctrines, if you probe it, measure it, and twist the words to read as you want them to, brood over them, hesitate, doubt, and then judge them according to your reason—that is not hearing the word or being its pupil. Then you are setting yourself up as its schoolmaster. In that way you will never discover the meaning of Christ's word or of his heavenly Father's will.

Simply hear what the Son of God says. Hear his word, and adhere to it. It is written: "Hear him!" To hear, to hear—that is the command, and thus we truly conform to God's will. He has promised to give the Holy Spirit to anyone who hears the Son, to enlighten and inflame one to understand that it is God's word. God will make a believer out of each one after his own heart. This he will surely do.

Sermons on the Gospel of St. John (1530-32)
LW 23, 229-30

"How beautiful are the feet of those who bring good news!"
—Romans 10:15b

n the first place, they are called "beautiful" because of their purity, because they do not preach the Gospel for personal advantage or empty glory, but only out of obedience to God as well as for the salvation of the hearers.

In the second place, the term "beautiful" according to the Hebrew idiom has more the meaning of something desirable or hoped for, something favored or worthy of love and affection. Thus the meaning is that the preaching of the Gospel is something lovable and desirable for those who are under the Law.

But what is meant by the term "feet"? According to the first interpretation, the term refers to the attitude and the devotion of those who preach, which must be free of all love of money and glory.

But according to the Hebrew, which is more accurate, the term "feet" can be taken in a literal sense, namely, that the coming of preachers of good things is something desirable for those who are tortured by sins and an evil conscience. And even more correctly the term can signify their very words themselves or the sound and the syllables, the pronunciation of the words of those who preach. For their voices are like feet or vehicles or wheels by which the word is carried or rolled or it walks to the ears of the hearers. Hence he says: "Their voice goes out through all the earth" (Ps. 19:4). And again: "His word runs swiftly" (Ps. 147:15). Whatever runs has feet: the word runs, therefore the word has feet, which are its pronunciations and its sounds. While the hearer sits quietly and receives the word, the "feet" of the preacher run over him.

Lectures on Romans (1515-16)
LW 25, 415-17

79

*Therefore, as the Holy Spirit says: "Today, if you hear
his voice, do not harden your hearts."*
—Hebrews 3:7-8a

One should note that this is the one, and the greatest, thing God requires of all people, that they hear his voice. Therefore Moses impresses so many times throughout Deuteronomy: "Hear, O Israel" and "If you hear the voice of the Lord your God." Indeed, nothing resounds in the prophets more frequently than "hear," "they did not hear," and "they were unwilling to hear." And rightly so, because without faith it is impossible for God to be with us (cf. Heb. 11:6), or to work, for he does everything through his word alone. Thus none are able to cooperate with him unless they adhere to the word.

But human nature recoils violently from this hearing. Therefore, those who rely on their own counsel and "do not wait for the counsel of the Lord" (cf. Ps. 106:13) harden their hearts to their own immeasurable harm and impede the work of God in themselves. For God works beyond strength, beyond perception, beyond intention, and beyond every thought.

From this one now understands who the people are who annoy, irritate, exasperate, and contradict, as Scripture rather frequently speaks of them, namely, the people who do not believe the word of God and are impatient of the work of God. They follow their master as long as they are aware of visible things to rely on. If these things fail, they fail, too. Therefore faith in Christ is an exceedingly arduous thing. It is a removal from everything one experiences within and without to the things one experiences neither within nor without, namely to the invisible, most high, and incomprehensible God.

"Lectures on Hebrews" (1517-18)
LW 29, 148-49

PRAYER

And Abraham said to God, "O that Ishmael might live in your sight!" God said, "No, but your wife Sarah shall bear you a son, and you shall name him Isaac."
—Genesis 17:18-19a

ONE MAY OBSERVE HERE THAT GOD ALWAYS GRANTS MORE THAN we are able to ask for or to understand. Accordingly, one should learn that those who want to pray properly should accustom themselves to pray with confidence and not to be deterred either by the greatness of the things to be granted or by the unworthiness of their praying.

There is a very beautiful example in Monica, the mother of Augustine [a fifth century bishop], who prayed for her son and asked for nothing else than that he be delivered from the foolish ideas of the Manichaeans and be baptized. Like an anxious mother, she also considered betrothing a girl to him if in this way he might be converted.

But the more she prayed, the more unyielding and stubborn her son became. But when the time had come for the anxious prayer to be heard (for God is wont to delay his help), Augustine is not only converted and baptized, but he devotes himself completely to the study of theology and becomes a teacher who shines in the church up to this day and teaches and instructs it.

Monica had never asked for this. She would have been satisfied to have her son delivered from his error and become a Christian. But God wants to give greater things than we are able to ask for, provided that we do not tire of praying.

Lectures on Genesis (1538)
LW 3, 157-60

She never left the temple but worshiped there
with fasting and prayer night and day.
—Luke 2:37b

nna prayed day and night, and this surely indicates, too, that she was awake. But this must not be understood to mean that she prayed and fasted day and night, without interruption. Naturally, she also had to eat, drink, sleep, and rest. The meaning is rather that such works made up her life; these were the things she did day and night. What a person does during the day and night must not therefore be understood to refer to the whole day and the whole night.

"Prayer," here is understood to be not only oral prayer, but everything the soul does in God's word—hearing, speaking, composing, meditating, and the like. Quite a few psalms are recited as prayers and yet in them scarcely three verses offer petitions. The other verses say and teach something; they punish sin, they invite us to talk with God, with ourselves, and with people. Such works were the service rendered to God by all the saints of old.

But our prayer today occurs solely in the babbling of words. Nobody thinks seriously to ask or receive something from God; rather prayer is undertaken as an obligation and one leaves it at that. They give no thought at all to the fact that they should serve God with prayer, that is, that they should pray for the common needs of Christendom. If they were to serve God and their neighbor with their praying they would not think of the number of psalms and individual words they had prayed. Rather they would think about how seriously they were seeking in these things God's honor and their neighbor's salvation, which is the true service of God. That would be true prayer and divine service like that of Anna.

Sermon on "The Gospel for the Sunday after Christmas, Luke 2[:33-40]"
(1522)
LW 52, 139-40

Before they call I will answer.
—Isaiah 65:24a

T his is a very lovely promise: "I will answer before they call." This promise is extremely necessary for strengthening our hearts and inciting them to pray. In the presence of God our prayers are regarded in such a way that they are answered before we call. The prayer of the righteous man is answered before it is finished. Before the prayer begins to formulate, while he is still speaking in general, it is answered as in Psalm 21:2: "Thou hast given him his heart's desire."

So Bernard [twelfth century French monk and mystic] says to his brothers: "Do not despise prayers, and know that as soon as you will have raised your voices, they are written in heaven, and it will come to pass and it will be given you. If it is not given, then it is not good for you, and God will give you something in its place that is better and more useful." This statement of Bernard comes from the Holy Spirit.

Thus if I pray, I am anticipating a great thing in my prayer. And our prayer pleases God; he requires it and delights in it. He promises, commands, and shapes it. God cannot get enough of the prayers of the godly. Therefore the prayer of the godly is likened to the most attractive odor that one cannot smell enough. Then he says: "I will hear."

Lectures on Isaiah (1527-30)
LW 17, 392-93

*And God, who searches the heart, knows what is the mind
of the Spirit, because the Spirit intercedes for the saints
according to the will of God.*
—Romans 8:27

Christian people are precious in God's sight and their prayer is powerful and great, for they have been sanctified by Christ's blood and anointed with the Spirit of God. Whatever they sincerely pray for, especially in the unexpressed yearning of their hearts, becomes a great, unbearable cry in God's ears. God must listen, as he did to Moses (Exod. 14:15). There God said, "Why do you cry to me?" even though Moses couldn't whisper, so great was his anxiety and trembling in the terrible troubles that beset him. Even Moses did not know how or for what he should pray—not knowing how the deliverance would be accomplished—but his cry came from his heart.

God intends that his promise and our prayer or yearning, which is grounded in that promise should not be disdained or rejected, but be highly valued and esteemed. Further, God accomplishes much through the faith and longing of another, even a stranger, even though there is still no personal faith. But this is given through the channel of another's intercession, as in the gospel Christ raised the widow's son at Nain because of the prayer of his mother apart from the faith of the son. And he freed the little daughter of the Canaanite woman from the demon through the faith of the mother apart from the daughter's faith.

"Comfort for Women Who Have Had a Miscarriage"(1542)
LW 43, 248, 250

Be constant in prayer.
—Romans 12:12 (Luther's translation)

T his is spoken in opposition to those who only read the Psalms without any heart. And we must be on our guard that the prayers in church in our day do not become more of a hindrance than a help. First, because we offend God more by reading them when our heart is not in it, as he says: "This people honors me with their lips . . ." (Matt. 15:8; Mark 7:6; Isa. 29:13). Second, because we are deceived and made secure by the appearance of these things, as if we had truly prayed properly. And thus we never become really attached to the desire for true prayer, but when we pray these things, we think that we have prayed and are in need of nothing more. This is a terrible danger.

This is the reason why he inserted the word "constant," a great watchword that must be noted and respected by all, and especially by clerics. For this word signifies that we must put real work into our praying. And it is not in vain. For as the ancient fathers have said, "There is no work like praying to God."

85

Therefore, when believers want to enter the priesthood, they must first consider that they are entering a work that is harder than any other, namely, the work of prayer. For this requires a subdued and broken mind and an elevated and victorious spirit.

Lectures on Romans (1515-16)
LW 25, 458

WORSHIP

These things I remember as I pour out my soul:
how I went with the throng, and led them in procession
to the house of God, with glad shouts and songs
of thanksgiving, a multitude keeping festival.
—Psalm 42:4

NOW THIS MULTITUDE MUST HAVE SOME KIND OF A ROOM AND ITS days or hours, which will be convenient for the listeners. Therefore God very wisely arranged and appointed things, and instituted the holy sacrament to be administered in the congregation at a place where we can come together, pray, and give thanks to God. Just as is done in worldly affairs when something that concerns the community must be dealt with, so much the more should this be done where we are to hear the word of God.

And here the advantage is that when Christians thus come together their prayers are twice as strong as otherwise. One can and one really should pray in every place and every hour; but prayer is nowhere so mighty and strong as when the whole multitude prays together. Thus the dear patriarchs [and matriarchs] gathered with their families, and anybody else who happened to be with them, under a tree, or put up a tent, and erected an altar, and this was their temple and house of God, where they talked about Christ, the coming seed who was promised to them, sacrificed together, called upon God, and gave thanks to him. And thus they were always glad to be with the multitude whenever they could, even though they also mediated upon God's word and promise and prayed by themselves in private.

"Sermon at the Dedication of the Castle Church in Torgau"(1544)
LW 51, 337-38

Observe the sabbath day and keep it holy,
as the LORD your GOD commanded you.
—Deuteronomy 5:12

What does it mean to "keep holy" a day? Obviously it does not mean to sit in idleness and do nothing. It means rather, in the first place, to do something on that day which is a holy work, which is owing only to God, namely, that above all other things one preaches God's word purely and holily, not as these scribes and Pharisees who falsify and pervert God's commandment. And likewise, that the others hear and learn God's word and help to see to it that it is purely preached and kept. That is what it means rightly to observe the day of rest and to "consecrate" the place or the church.

Secondly, it means that we receive the word of God, which we have heard in our hearts and with which we have thus been sprinkled, in order that it may bring forth power and fruit in us, and that we may publicly confess it and intend to hold onto it through life and through death.

87

Thirdly, it means that when we have heard God's word we also lift up to God our common, united incense, that is, that we call upon him and pray to him together (which we know is certainly pleasing and acceptable to him, particularly in common assembly), and also praise and thank God together with joy for all his benefits, temporal and eternal, and all the wonderful works he does in his church. Thus everything that is done in such an assembly of the whole congregation or church is nothing but holy, godly business and work and is a holy sabbath, in order both that God may be rightly and holily served and all people be helped.

"Sermon at the Dedication of the Castle Church in Torgau"(1544)
LW 51, 342-43

At that time people began to invoke the name of the LORD.
—Genesis 4:26b

By worship of God, Moses does not mean the ceremonies devised and handed down by men, not the statues that have been set up or other playthings of human reason, but calling upon the name of "the Lord." Here, then, we have the highest form of worship, which is pleasing to God and later on was commanded in the First Table of the Ten Commandments, and which included the fear of God, trust in God, confession, prayer, and preaching.

The First Commandment demands faith, that you believe that God is a helper in due time, as Psalm 9:9 declares. The second demands confession and prayer, that we call upon the name of God in danger and give thanks to God. The third, that we teach the truth and defend and preserve sound doctrine. These are the true and only forms of worship of God that God demands; he does not demand sacrifices, money, and other things. He demands the First Table, that you hear, meditate on, and teach the word; that you pray, and that you fear God. Whenever this is done, there will follow spontaneously, as it were, the forms of worship or the works of the Second Table. It is impossible for one who worships in accordance with the First Table not to keep the Second Table also.

Lectures on Genesis (1535-36)
LW 1, 328-29

For six days you shall continue to eat unleavened bread,
and on the seventh day there shall be a solemn assembly
for the LORD your God, when you shall do no work.
—Deuteronomy 16:8

Human nature tends unceasingly to set up ceremonies and institute forms for worshiping God. Therefore it is necessary that it be curbed and kept in the word of God, through which we are sure that what we do is divinely instituted and pleases God. The Old Testament festivals also assure that the people come together at least two or three times a year, hear and learn the Law of God, and be kept in the unity of faith and life.

There are, however, three things that he wanted remembered at these three festivals. In the Festival of Passover they should recall the Exodus from Egypt. At the Pentecost Festival they should remember receiving the Law on Mt. Sinai. At the Feast of Tabernacles they were to remember all the physical benefits shown in those forty years in the desert. So you see that the festivals are established for the sake of our salvation and the glory of God, that the word of God may be heard and his blessings remembered, that we may be instructed, nourished, and preserved in faith and love.

89

All these festivals we celebrate by an allegory of the Spirit in one festival. For we observe the Passover every day when we proclaim and believe that Christ, the Lamb of God, was offered up for us. So daily we have Pentecost when we receive the new Law, the Spirit, into our hearts (Jer. 31:33) through the ministry of the word. Daily we celebrate the Feast of Tabernacles when we teach and experience that we are strangers in this world and sojourn in the tabernacles of our bodies, which last but a short time.

Lectures on Deuteronomy (1523-25)
LW 9, 156-57

But the Lord answered her, "Martha, Martha,
you are worried and distracted by many things;
there is need of only one thing. Mary has chosen
the better part, which will not be taken away from her."
—Luke 10:41-42

Other matters concerning worship will adjust themselves as the need arises. This is the sum of the matter: Let everything in the worship service be done so that the word may have free course instead of the prattling and rattling that has been the rule up to now. We can spare everything except the word. Again, we profit by nothing as much as by the word. For the whole Scripture shows that the word should have free course among Christians. In Luke 10:42, Christ himself says, "One thing is needful," meaning that Mary sit at the feet of Christ and hear his word daily. This is the best part to choose and it shall not be taken away forever. It is an eternal word. Everything else must pass away, no matter how much care and trouble it may give Martha. God help us achieve this. Amen.

"Concerning the Order of Public Worship" (1523)
LW 53, 14

GOOD WORKS

"I give you a new commandment, that you love one another. Just as I have loved you, you also should love one another. By this everyone will know that you are my disciples, if you have love for one another."
—*John 13:34-35*

To believers no law is given by which they become righteous before God, as St. Paul says in 1 Timothy 1:9, because they are alive and righteous and saved by faith. Believers need nothing further except to prove their faith by works. Truly, if faith is there, they cannot hold back; they prove themselves, break out into good works, confess and teach this gospel before the people, and stake their lives on it. Everything that they live and do is directed to their neighbor's profit, in order to help the neighbor—not only to attainment of this grace, but also in body, property, and honor. Seeing that Christ has done this for them, they thus follow Christ's example.

That is what Christ meant when at the last he gave no other commandment than love, by which people were to know who were his disciples and true believers. For where works and love do not break forth, there faith is not right, the gospel does not yet take hold, and Christ is not rightly known.

"Prefaces to the New Testament" (1522, revised 1546)
LW 35, 361

"Let your light shine before others, so that they may see your good works and give glory to your Father in heaven."
—Matthew 5:16

What he calls "good works" here is the exercise, expression, and confession of the teaching about Christ and faith, and the suffering for its sake. He is talking about works by which we "shine." This shining is the real job of believing or teaching, by which we also help others to believe. These are the works whose necessary consequence must be "that the heavenly Father is honored and praised."

Matthew is not writing about ordinary works that people should do for one another out of love, which he talks about in Matthew 25:35ff. Rather he is thinking principally about the distinctly Christian work of teaching correctly, of stressing faith, and of showing how to strengthen and preserve it. This is how we testify that we really are Christians. The other works are not such a reliable criterion, for even sham Christians can put on the adornment of big, beautiful works of love.

Thus the most reliable index to a true Christian is this: from the way he praises and preaches Christ the people learn that they are nothing and Christ is everything. It is the kind of work that cannot remain hidden. It has to shine and let itself be seen publicly. That is always why it alone is persecuted, for the world can tolerate other works. This also entitles it to be called a work through which our Father is recognized and praised.

These are the works that should be first and foremost. They should be followed by those pertaining to our relations with our neighbor in what are called "works of love," which shine, too, but only insofar as they are ignited and sustained by faith.

Commentary on "The Sermon on the Mount" (1532)
LW 21, 65-66

How can we escape if we neglect so great a salvation?
—Hebrews 2:3a

I n the Law there are very many works—they are all external—but in the Gospel there is only one work—it is internal—which is faith. Therefore the works of the Law bring about external righteousness; the works of faith bring about righteousness that is hidden in God.

Consequently, when the Jews asked in John 6:28, "What must we do, to be doing the works of God?" Christ draws them away from a large number of works and reduces the works to one. He says: "This is the work of God, that you believe in him whom he has sent" (John 6:29). Therefore, the whole substance of the new law and its righteousness is that one and only faith in Christ.

Yet it is not so one-and-only and so sterile as human opinions are, for Christ lives. Not only lives but works, and not only works but reigns. Therefore it is impossible for faith in him to be idle. It is alive, and it itself works and triumphs, and in this way works flow forth spontaneously from faith.

For in this way our patience flows from the patience of Christ, and our humility from his, and the other good works in like manner, provided that we believe firmly that he has done all these things for us, not only for us but also before our eyes, that is as St. Augustine is wont to say, not only as a sacrament but also as an example.

"Lectures on Hebrews"(1517-18)
LW 29, 123

93

Rescue the weak and the needy;
deliver them from the hand of the wicked.
—Psalm 82:4

Who is the person at whose door and into whose house such good works do not present themselves every day? There is no need for him to travel far or inquire about good works.

But you might ask, "Why does God not do it all by himself, because he is able to help everyone and knows how to help everyone?" Yes, he can do it; but he does not want to do it alone. He wants us to work with him. He does us the honor of wanting to effect his work with us and through us. And if we are not willing to accept such honor, he will, after all, do the work alone, and help the poor. And those who were not willing to help him and who despised the great honor of doing his work he will condemn along with the unrighteous as those who made common cause with the unrighteous. Although he alone is blessed, he does us the honor of wanting to share his blessedness with us.

"Treatise on Good Works" (1520)
LW 44, 51-52

You shall not steal.
—Exodus 20:15

his commandment also has a work that includes very many good works while opposing many vices. In German, this work is called "selflessness," a willingness to help and serve all people with one's own means.

It was not in vain that the wise man said, "Happy is the rich man who is found without blemish, who has not run after gold, and has not set his confidence in the treasures of money. Who is he? We will praise him because he has performed a miracle in his life" (Eccles. 31:8-9). Yes, there certainly are very few who notice and recognize such lust for gold in themselves. For greed can have a very pretty and attractive cover for its shame; it is called provision for the body and the needs of nature. Under this cover greed insatiably amasses unlimited wealth.

But if the heart expects and puts its trust in divine favor, how can a person be greedy and anxious? Such people are absolutely certain that they are acceptable to God: therefore, they do not cling to money; they use their money cheerfully and freely for the benefit of their neighbor.

In fact, in this commandment it can clearly be seen that all good works must be done in faith and proceed from faith. People are generous because they trust God and never doubt but that they will always have enough. In contrast, people are covetous and anxious because they do not trust God. Now faith is the master workman and the motivating force behind the good works of generosity, just as it is in all the other commandments.

"Treatise on Good Works"(1520)
LW 44, 106-9

Our Mission to Others

"This is my commandment, that you love one another
as I have loved you. . . . You are my friends
if you do what I command you."
—John 15:12, 14

IT IS SURELY KIND AND PLEASING THAT CHRIST CALLS THEM HIS friends. For he would like to encourage and rouse us to pay heed to his love, to consider how he made the Father our friend and how he proved himself our friend above all friends. But all of us who are his friends must also live in friendship with one another.

Thus he gives this kind commandment. The Lord, who gave body and soul and did everything for us, does not demand of us payment for this as though we had to do so for his sake. He asks that we do something in our own interest. From him we have everything for nothing, and all that is required of us is that we help one another.

Christ says: "I ask you to love one another, to be loyally attached to one another, and to serve one another in a friendly way—all this in your own best interest. I am commanding you to do nothing more than to love one another as I have loved you. After all, it is only natural for you to do this, and it should be done spontaneously."

For it is natural—and everybody must admit this—that everyone would like to be shown love, fidelity, and help. Therefore we have been intermingled by God in order that we may live side by side and serve and help one another. God has no need whatever of such service and help, nor does he give this command for his sake. But we, of course, need it in our inmost hearts.

Sermons on the Gospel of St. John (1537)
LW 24, 251-53

For the whole law is summed up in a single commandment,
"You shall love your neighbor as yourself."
—Galatians 5:14

Love is the highest virtue. It is neither called forth by anything that someone deserves nor deterred by what is undeserving and ungrateful. And no creature toward which you should practice love is nobler than your neighbor—that is, any human being especially one who needs your help.

This person is not a devil, not a lion or a bear, not a stone or a log. This is a living creature very much like you. There is nothing living on earth that is more lovable or more necessary. The neighbor is naturally suited for a civilized and social existence. Thus nothing could be regarded as worthier of love in the whole universe than our neighbor.

But such is the amazing craft of the devil that he is able not only to remove this noble object of love from my mind but even to persuade my heart of the exactly opposite opinion. My heart regards the neighbor as worthy, not of love but of the bitterest hatred. The devil accomplishes this very easily, suggesting to me: "Look, this person suffers from such and such a fault. The neighbor has chided you, has done you damage." Immediately this most lovable of objects becomes vile. My neighbor no longer seems to be someone who should be loved, but an enemy deserving of bitter hatred.

In this way we are transformed from lovers into haters. All that is left to us of this commandment are the naked and meaningless letters and syllables: "You shall love your neighbor as yourself."

Lectures on Galatians (1535)
LW 27, 58

"In everything do to others what you would have them do to you; for this is the law and the prophets."
—Matthew 7:12

 ith these words Christ concludes the teaching he has been giving in the Sermon on the Mount. He wraps it all up in a little package where it can all be found. Thus everyone can put it in his bosom and keep it.

It is as if he were saying: "Would you like to know what I have been preaching, and what Moses and all the Prophets teach you? I shall tell it to you so briefly and put it in such a way that you dare not complain about its being too long or too hard to remember." This is the kind of sermon that can be expanded or contracted. From it all teaching and preaching go forth and are broadcast, and here they come back together. How could it be put more succinctly and clearly than in these words?

The trouble is that the world and our old Adam refuse to let us ponder what he says and measure our lives against the standard of this teaching. We let it go in one ear and out the other. If we always measured our lives and actions against this standard, we would not be so coarse and heedless in what we do, but we would always have enough to do. We could become our own teachers, teaching ourselves what we ought to do.

Commentary on "The Sermon on the Mount" (1532)
LW 21, 235

For you say, "I am rich, I have prospered, and I need nothing."
You do not realize that you are wretched,
pitiable, poor, blind, and naked.
—Revelation 3:17

t is the worst kind of vice and the most demonic kind of pride for us to commend ourselves and pat ourselves on the back if we see or feel some special gift in ourselves. We do not thank God for it, but we become so proud and contemptuous of others and so preoccupied with it that we do not pay attention to whatever else we are doing, and imagine that we are in fine shape. We rob God of his glory this way, and we make ourselves an idol, without seeing the trouble we cause by all this. Look at what the Apocalypse says to a bishop who let himself think that he was more learned and better than others (Rev. 3:17).

If it is true that your gift is greater than somebody else's, this is as it must be, because your office is different, higher, and greater. But when you go on to use your gift as a mirror in which to admire yourself, you spoil it completely and make this sublime ornament filthier than everybody else's faults. The richer your gifts, the more abominable the perversion if you make them an idol. Thus you replace God with yourself in your own heart. You become arrogant toward your neighbor and so completely blind in everything that you can no longer know or see God or your neighbor or even yourself.

God did not give you your gifts for you to tickle yourself with them, but for you to help your neighbor with them when he needs it, and thus by your strength to bear his weakness, by your piety and honor to cover up his sin and to conceal his shame, as God through Christ has done for you and still does every day.

Commentary on "The Sermon on the Mount" (1532)
LW 21, 216-18

*Thieves must give up stealing; rather let them labor
and work honestly with their own hands, so as to have
something to share with the needy.
—Ephesians 4:28*

 umans do not live for themselves alone in these mortal bodies to work for their bodies alone, but they live also for all of humanity on earth; rather, they live only for others and not for themselves. They cannot ever in this life be idle and without works toward their neighbors.

People, however, need none of these things for their righteousness and salvation. Therefore they should be guided in all their works by this thought and contemplate this one thing alone, that they may serve and benefit others in all that they do, considering nothing except the need and the advantage of their neighbors. Accordingly the Apostle commands us to work with our hands so that we may give to the needy, although he might have said that we should work to support ourselves.

This is what makes caring for the body a Christian work, that through its health and comfort we may be able to work, to acquire, and lay by funds with which to aid those who are in need, that in this way the strong member may serve the weaker, and we may be children of God, each caring for and working for the other, bearing one another's burdens and so fulfilling the law of Christ (Gal. 6:2). This is a truly Christian life. Here faith is truly active through love.

"The Freedom of a Christian"(1520)
LW 31, 364-65

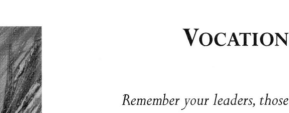

VOCATION

Remember your leaders, those who spoke
the word of God to you; consider the outcome
of their way of life, and imitate their faith.
—Hebrews 13:7

IN GOD'S SIGHT THIS PRINCIPLE STANDS FIRM AND UNSHAKABLE: all saints live by the same Spirit and by the same faith, and are guided and governed by the same Spirit and the same faith, but they all do different external works. For God does not work through them at the same time, in the same place, in the same work, or in the sight of the same people. He moves at different times, in different places, in different works, and in different people, but he always rules them by the same Spirit and in the same faith.

And each one is compelled by the work, place, time, persons, and circumstances, previously unknown to him, to follow God as he rules and guides him. This is the true knowledge of faith in which all saints are instructed, each one in his own vocation.

Treatise on "The Judgment of Martin Luther on Monastic Vows" (1521)
LW 44, 269

There was also a prophet, Anna . . . She was of a great age,
having lived with her husband seven years after her
marriage, then as a widow to the age of eighty-four.
She never left the temple but worshiped there with fasting
and prayer night and day.
—Luke 2:36-37

It is a rather dangerous thing, if one looks only at the works and not at the person or station or calling. It is most unpleasing to God for someone to give up the duties of one's calling or station and to want to take up the works of the saints. Hence if a married woman should want to follow Anna and would forsake husband and children, house and parents, in order to go on a pilgrimage, to pray, to fast, and to go to church, she would only tempt God. To leave one's own calling and to attach oneself to alien undertakings, surely amounts to walking on one's ears and to turning everything upside down. Good works must be performed, and one should pray and fast to the extent that the work of one's calling and station are not neglected or impeded. Serving God is not tied to one or two works, nor is it confined to one or two callings, but it is distributed over all works and all callings.

Luke also writes that Anna lived seven years with her husband. By this expression he praises her married state and the duties of this estate also, so that nobody should get the idea that he considers only praying and fasting good works. For she did not do this while she was living with her husband, but only after she had become a lonely widow.

You, likewise, must pay attention to your estate; you will find enough good works to do, if you wish to be pious. Every estate has enough works without needing to look for strange ones.

Sermon on "The Gospel for the Sunday after Christmas,
Luke 2[:33-40]" (1522)
LW 52, 124-25

[Hagar] gave this name to the LORD who spoke to her:
"You are the God who sees me," for she said,
"I have now seen the One who sees me."
—Genesis 16:13 (NIV)

The word of God is never without fruit. Therefore the rebellious, proud, and disobedient Hagar is changed when the angel speaks. She returns to her mistress and patiently submits to her authority. Not only this; she acknowledges God's mercy, praises God, and calls upon him by a new name in order to proclaim abroad the kindness through which he had manifested himself to her.

This example is profitable for giving us instruction in order that all may come to know the kindnesses of God in their vocations, may be thankful for them and proclaim them. Likewise, that we may bear with patience the chastisements inflicted by our superiors, because God takes pleasure in such patience and sends help.

It is a sacrifice of thanksgiving and a service most pleasing to God if you acknowledge and proclaim his acts of kindness and call him he who sees me as if you were saying: "I thought I had been completely forsaken by God. But now I see that he had regard for me and did not cast me aside when I was in trouble."

This is a most beautiful name for God. Would that we all could bestow it on him. We would conclude with certainty that he has regard for us and cares for us, especially when he seems to have forgotten us. For he who can say in affliction: "God sees me" has true faith and can do and bear everything, yes, he overcomes all things and is triumphant.

103

Lectures on Genesis (1538)
LW 3, 69-70

"Blessed are those who mourn, for they will be comforted."
—Matthew 5:4

Mourning and sorrow are not a rare plant among Christians, in spite of outward appearances. Daily, whenever they look at the world, they must see and feel in their heart so much wickedness, arrogance, contempt, and blasphemy of God and his word, so much sorrow and sadness, which the devil causes in both the spiritual and the secular realm. Therefore they cannot have many joyful thoughts, and their spiritual joy is very weak. If they were to look at this continually and did not turn their eyes away from time to time, they could not be happy for a moment.

Simply begin to be a Christian, and you will soon find out what it means to mourn and be sorrowful. If you can do nothing else, then get married, settle down, and make a living in faith. Love the word of God, and do what is required of you in your station. Then you will experience, both from your neighbors and in your own household, that things will not go as you might wish. You will be hindered and hemmed in on every side, so that you will suffer enough and see enough to make your heart sad. But especially the dear preachers must learn this well and be disciplined daily with all sorts of envy, hatred, scorn, ridicule, ingratitude, contempt, and blasphemy. In addition, they have to stew inside, so that their heart and soul is pierced through and continually tormented.

Those who mourn this way are entitled to have fun and to take it wherever they can so that they do not completely collapse for sorrow. Christ also adds these words and promises this consolation so that they do not despair in their sorrow nor let the joy of their heart be taken away and extinguished altogether, but mix this mourning with comfort and refreshment.

Commentary on "The Sermon on the Mount" (1532)
LW 21, 20-21

"Ask for whatever you wish, and it will be done for you."
—*John 15:7b*

Open your mouth confidently, as a little child speaks to its father, who is pleased with everything it does if only it comes to him. The father is especially glad to comply with all the child's requests if it chats with him in a childlike manner when it asks him for something. Not only that, but he also provides for the child, and his one concern is to supply all the child's needs.

Hence Christians enjoy a great and glorious advantage if they remain pure and firm in the faith and guard against false doctrine and impure living. This is a splendid and comforting sermon on the estate of being a Christian.

Where is there a calling or walk of life on earth about which there are so many splendid promises as about this one? And these promises pertain to all who are called Christians and are baptized, whether monk or layperson, master or servant, mistress or maid, young or old. This must indeed be an estate blessed and prized above all others, to which the divine promise is assured that whatever those in it ask of and desire from God shall surely be granted and shall be yea and amen before God. Besides, everything that is done in this estate shall be approved and praised by God. Should we not be willing to wander to the ends of the earth in search of such a promise? Now it is carried before our very door without any toil or cost on our part, for the benefit of all who will accept it.

Sermons on the Gospel of St. John (1537)
LW 24, 239-40

STRENGTH IN WEAKNESS

*The LORD says to my lord, "Sit at my right hand
until I make your enemies your footstool."*
—Psalm 110:1

OBSERVE THIS FOR YOUR COMFORT: HERE THESE ENEMIES ARE never called our enemies, but enemies of the Lord Christ. "Your enemies," he says, although they really attack Christendom and Christians must suffer, as it actually happens. For Christ cannot be attacked. They cannot hurt one hair on his head, much less drag him down from his throne. Still they are properly called his enemies, not ours.

For the world and the devil do not attack and plague us because we have merited or caused it. The only reason for it is that we believe this Lord and confess his word. For this reason he must deal with them as enemies who attacks his person. Everything that happens to the individual Christian, such as the terrors of sin, anxiety and grief of the heart, torture, or death, he regards as though it happened to him. He also says through the prophet Zechariah (Zech. 2:8): "He who touches you touches the apple of my eye." And in Matthew 25:40 we read: "As you did it to one of the least of these my brethren, you did it to me."

Though we may feel the terrors of sin, anxiety and grief of heart, torture, and death, we are to remember that these are not our enemies but the enemies of our Lord, who is of our flesh and blood. We are to view him as the enemy of our enemies. In this comfort we are to direct them away from ourselves to Christ: "Do you not know? God has already judged you and pronounced you the footstool of Christ."

Commentary on "Psalm 110" (1535)
LW 13, 262

In returning and rest you shall be saved; in quietness
and in trust shall be your strength.
—Isaiah 30:15b

Translate it thus: "If you will sit down and be quiet, you shall be saved. Do not lose heart and do not lose your temper. Wait till the storm blows over and keep still." Now that is a marvelous victory, to conquer by sitting and waiting! Meanwhile the flesh runs and toils and looks for help.

But trust in God, be patient, and commit everything to him. In a wonderful way you will see God as your protector. This passage is, therefore, an outstanding, golden, and magnificent promise: "In sitting quietly you shall be saved." Be calm, wait, wait, commit your cause to God, he will make it succeed. Look for him a little at a time; wait, wait. But because this waiting seems long to the flesh and appears like death, the flesh always wavers. But keep faith. Patience will overcome wickedness.

The prophet further impresses this when he says: "Blessed are all those who wait for him" (Isa. 30:18). That is to say, they who wait for God are the holy, the good, and the godly. These wait for God, even when he takes his time. Therefore the blessed are saved. Everything would turn out all right, if you could only wait. Therefore, in all trouble let us wait for God and we shall be blessed.

107

Lectures on Isaiah (ca. 1528)
LW 16, 258-61

*Have you not known? Have you not heard? The LORD is
the everlasting God, the Creator of the ends of the earth.
He does not faint or grow weary.*
—Isaiah 40:28

This is a wonderful proclamation concerning God—he does not faint or grow weary. This seems mad to reason. But the prophet is depicting God in terms of our senses, as if he were saying: "We get tired and are worn out by Satan's plotting and cunning tricks. But you have a God who does not get tired. He will set you free from the incessant stratagems of Satan." Satan and the world are our relentless enemies. They keep after us until at last they exhaust us.

Therefore God consoles those who labor and are wearied: "I will not become weary. I have always been active, I am fresh and new. I can help you." Remembering this a certain nun by the name of Mechtild kept repelling the onslaughts of Satan with one word: "I am a Christian."

So I, too, must say: "I am dead, but Christ lives; I am a sinner, but Christ is righteous. I believe in Jesus Christ and was baptized in his name." Thus when we are fatigued, let us run to the fresh and untiring Christ and not remain with ourselves.

Lectures on Isaiah (1527-30)
LW 17, 30

Strengthen the weak hands.
—Isaiah 35:3a

This is a wonderful comfort that is to be understood not in a physical but in an internal sense, because it shines under the appearance of the cross. The members of the church are exposed to all, to Satan and to the craftiness and power of the world and the flesh. Therefore the prophet comforts them with exceedingly great consolations.

Strengthen the weak hands, he commands. Give medicine to those hands that are so weary, so that you become strong again. For Satan has two ways of fighting. He would gladly cast the faithful down suddenly from their joy and faith and into fear and despair. Secondly, he cunningly strives by long lasting torments and by the unremitting pressure of the torments to tire them out. These attacks are extremely powerful, and against Satan's continuous attack we must set our continuous divine help. The devil is a spirit at leisure and thinks of nothing but to take us by storm. We ought not have slack and idle hands over against his deceptions.

We ought to strengthen ourselves with these words and say, "Though all devils were rolled into one, my God is still greater." The afflicted must be comforted with such spiritual consolations of the word, not with fleshly comfort which does nothing for troubled consciences. With spiritual comfort and with the living word of God, the afflicted are made strong.

Lectures on Isaiah (ca. 1528)
LW 16, 300-1

He gives power to the faint.
—*Isaiah 40:29a*

Here you must understand what it means to be faint and impotent, in opposition to carnal reason, which wants to be strong and most powerful. Reason willingly hears one thing—that God gives strength, but it does not want to be worn out and nothing. So all the self-righteous willingly receive strength from God, but they do not want to be faint, as if God would not give strength to the weary. What need is there for the secure to receive strength?

But God gives strength to the weary, the oppressed, and the troubled. The emphasis lies on the word "faint," but we look for the stress on the word "power." It is as if God were saying: "You must be weary and emptied, so that there is no way out for you. Then I will give you strength. First you must become nothing, then consolation and strength will come."

Therefore let us learn to console ourselves when we are afflicted and say, "What I do not have and what I cannot do, that Christ has and can do."

Lectures on Isaiah (1527-30)
LW 17, 31

SAINT AND SINNER

Greet every saint in Christ Jesus.
—Philippians 4:21a

THE HOLY SCRIPTURES CALL CHRISTIANS SAINTS AND THE people of God. It's a pity that it's forgotten that we are saints, for to forget this is to forget Christ and Baptism.

You say that the sins we commit every day offend God, and therefore we are not saints. To this I reply: Mother love is stronger than the filth and scabbiness on a child, and so the love of God toward us is stronger than the dirt that clings to us. Accordingly, although we are sinners, we do not lose our filial relation on account of our filthiness, nor do we fall from grace on account of our sin.

"Table Talk Recorded by Veit Dietrich" (1533)
LW 54, 70

*And Ham, the father of Canaan, saw the nakedness
of his father, and told his two brothers outside.*
—Genesis 9:22

All this serves for our instruction. Because at times God permits even righteous and holy persons to stumble and fall either into actual offenses or into such as seem so, we must be on our guard lest we immediately pass judgment, as Ham did. He had despised his father long since, but only now does he do so openly. Moreover, he maintains that his father is feeble-minded from senility and has evidently been forsaken by the Holy Spirit, because he, on whom lay the rule of the church, state, and the home, has not refrained from drunkenness. But, O wretched Ham, how happy you are that now at last you have found what you were seeking, namely poison in a lovely rose!

God should be praised and blessed forever for dealing with his saints in a truly wonderful manner. For while he permits them to be weak and to stumble, while he lets them abound with actions that result in displeasure and offense, and the world judges and condemns them, he forgives them these weaknesses and has compassion on them. On the other hand, he leaves to Satan and utterly rejects those who are angels in their own eyes.

Hence when we see saints fall, let us not be offended. Much less let us gloat over the weakness of other people, or rejoice, as though we were stronger, wiser, and holier. Rather let us bear with and cover, and even extenuate and excuse, such mistakes as much as we can, bearing in mind that what the other person has experienced today we may perhaps experience tomorrow. We are all one mass, and we are all born of one flesh.

Lectures on Genesis (ca. 1536)
LW 2, 169, 171

The disagreement became so sharp that they parted company.
—Acts 15:39a

P aul and Barnabas had been set aside for the ministry of the Gospel among the Gentiles and had traveled through many areas and announced the Gospel. Yet Luke testified that there came such a sharp disagreement between them that they parted company. Here there was a fault either in Paul or in Barnabas. It must have been a very sharp disagreement to separate such close companions, and this is what the text suggests. Such examples are written for our comfort. For it is a great comfort for us to hear that even such great saints sin—a comfort those who say that saints cannot sin would take away from us.

Samson, David, and many other celebrated leaders who were full of the Holy Spirit fell into huge sins. Such errors and sins of the saints are set forth in order that those who are troubled and desperate may find comfort and that those who are proud may be afraid. No one has ever fallen so grievously as to not have stood up again. On the other hand, no one has such a sure footing that he or she cannot fall. If Peter fell, I, too, may fall; if he stood up again, so can I.

Lectures on Galatians (1535)
LW 26, 108-9

113

So I find it to be a law that when I want to do
what is good, evil lies close at hand.
—Romans 7:21

St. Cyprian, in a sermon on the sickness unto death, finds here his comfort when thinking of his sins and says, "Ceaselessly, we must fight against avarice, unchastity, anger, and ambition. Steadfastly and with toil and sorrow we must wrestle with carnal desires and the enticements of the world. The human mind, surrounded and besieged by the assaults of the devil, can scarcely meet or resist them all. If avarice is prostrated, unchastity springs up. If lust is overcome, ambition takes its place. If ambition is despised, then anger is provoked, pride puffs up, drunkenness takes the offensive, hatred breaks the bonds of unity, jealousy breaks up friendship. The human spirit must suffer many persecutions and the heart must expect many perils."

Let us understand this properly! Believers cannot pray against sin and about sin or have such a desire to be free from sin, unless they are already godly. Only the Spirit who in Baptism has just begun his work and incipient grace are so constituted that they work against the sin that remains. Believers would like to be altogether godly, but cannot achieve this because of the resistance of the flesh. But those who have never begun to be godly do not struggle or lament or pray against their flesh and sin. They feel no resistance, but go on and follow where the flesh leads.

"Defense and Explanation on All the Articles" (1521)
LW 32, 22-23

Those who eat my flesh and drink my blood
abide in me, and I in them.
—John 6:56

Christ wants to indicate that many people have heard him, can converse about him, and cling to him so long as all goes well. But to remain with him, to abide in him and make their dwelling in him, to confess him with heart and lips when it really counts—that is no child's play or trifle. The true presence and greatness of faith are evinced when a person in the midst of life's storms neither speaks nor acts differently from the way the Christ who is in him speaks and acts. This is something that transcends human strength and human work.

Outwardly Christians stumble and fall from time to time. Only weakness and shame appear on the surface, revealing that the Christians are sinners who do that which displeases the world. Then they are regarded as fools, as Cinderellas, as footmats for the world, as damned, impotent, and worthless people. But this does not matter. In their weakness, sin, folly, and frailty there abides inwardly and secretly a force and power unrecognizable by the world and hidden from its view, but one which, for all that, carries off the victory; for Christ resides in them and manifests himself to them. I have seen many of these who, externally, tottered along very feebly, but when it came to the test and they faced the court, Christ bestirred himself in them, and they became so staunch that the devil had to flee.

Sermons on the Gospel of St. John (1530-32)
LW 23, 145-47

COMFORT

[The LORD] shielded him, cared for him,
guarded him as the apple of his eye.
—Deuteronomy 32:10b

NEVER DO WE FEEL THE HAND OF GOD MORE CLOSELY UPON US
than when we remember the years of our past life. St. Augustine
says, "If people were given the choice between dying and reliv-
ing their past life, they would surely choose death, seeing the
great dangers and evils which they had so narrowly escaped."
When considered rightly, this statement is very true.

Here people may see how often they have done and suffered
many things without effort or care of their own, yes, even without or against their own will. They gave little thought to them
before they occurred or while they were happening. Only after
all was over did they find themselves compelled to exclaim in
great surprise, "How did these things happen to me, when I gave
no thought to them, or thought something very different?" This
bears out the proverb, "The human mind proposes, but God dis-
poses" (Prov. 16:9). That is, God turns things around and brings
to pass something different from that which people had
planned. Thus it is not possible for us to deny that our lives and
actions are under the guidance, not of our prudence, but of the
wonderful power, wisdom, and goodness of God. Here we see
how often God was with us when we neither saw nor sensed it.

Therefore, even if there were no books or sermons, our
very own lives, led through so many evils and dangers, would, if
considered properly, abundantly commend to us the ever present and most tender goodness of God, which, far beyond our
thought and feeling, carried us in its bosom.

"Fourteen Consolations" (1520)
LW 42, 130-31

Hide me in the shadow of your wings.
—Psalm 17:8b

he shadow of your wings in a mystical sense is faith in Christ, which in this life is mysterious and shadowy. But the wings of Christ are his hands stretched out on the cross. For just as the body of Christ on the cross produces a shadow, so it casts a spiritual shadow on the soul, namely faith in his cross, under which every saint is protected.

Second, the shadow of the wings is the protection and watch of the holy angels or of contemplative people, who are the wings of God, for in them he soars and dwells in affectionate and encaptured minds.

Third, the shadow of the wings is the learning of the Scriptures, in which there is rest for those who devote themselves to this learning. Thus the bride says in Song of Solomon 2:3: "I sat down under his shadow, whom I desired."

First Lectures on the Psalms I (1513-15)
LW 10, 111

You are the most handsome of men;
grace is poured upon your lips.
—Psalm 45:2a

he poet has diligently read the prophecies and promises regarding Christ. He has seen that Christ's lips are the sweetest and loveliest lips, which attract the hearts of all the weak.

He does not call them simply "gracious" lips, but lips "overflowing with grace," in order to point out that Christ is superabundant in his lips. From his mouth, as from some overflowing fountain, the richest promises and teachings stem, and with these he strengthens and comforts souls.

Grace is on the lips of this king. Not only that, it overflows, so that you may understand how abundantly this fountain of grace flows and gushes forth. It is as though the psalmist said: "Our king has wisdom such as no one has, namely, the sweetest and loveliest wisdom. He helps the penitent, comforts the afflicted, recalls the despairing, raises up the fallen and humiliated, justifies sinners, gives life to the dying."

Christ himself says in Isaiah 50:4: "The Lord has given me the tongue of those who are taught, that I may know how to sustain with a word the one that is weary."

So mark this well. The tongue of Christ is not the kind that terrifies or hurts, except when he speaks to the proud and obstinate. This psalm speaks of the work that he exercises toward his own. Here nothing is heard but the voice of comfort for the lowly, the voice of joy, and the voice of the bridegroom.

118

Commentary on "Psalm 45" (1532)
LW 12, 211-12

Trust in him at all times, O people; pour out your heart
before him; God is a refuge for us.
—Psalm 62:8

ope in God, for he will not let you down. Others laugh, comfort, and make promises, but do not pin your hopes on them. Do not depend on them, for both their strength and their courage are uncertain. Strength fades, courage fails; God remains firm. In times of adversity and in times of prosperity, therefore, you may depend on God.

If you are lacking something, well, here is good advice: "Pour out your heart before him." Voice your complaint freely, and do not conceal anything from him. Regardless of what it is, just throw it in a pile before him, as you open your heart completely to a good friend. He wants to hear it, and he wants to give you his aid and counsel. Do not be bashful before him and do not think that what you ask is too big or too much. Come right out with it, even if all you have are bags full of need. Out with everything; God is greater and more able and more willing than all our transgressions. Do not dribble your requests before him; God is not a person whom you can overburden with your begging and asking. The more you ask, the happier he is to hear you. Only pour it all out, do not dribble or drip it. For he will not drip or dribble either, for he will flood you with a veritable deluge.

"God is a refuge for us," our hiding place, he and no one else.

Commentary on "The Four Psalms of Comfort" (1526)
LW 14, 237-38

"Do not let your hearts be troubled."
—*John 14:1a*

Christ knows that if we want to remain his own and adhere to Baptism, the Sacrament, and the Gospel, the devil will inevitably be our enemy, incessantly pressing us with all his might and contending for our body and soul. Even if God wards him off and prevents him from killing you in one day, he will nevertheless craftily and cunningly persist in trying at least to rob you of your courage and security. He will try to fill you with disquietude and sadness, and subsequently to bring you into other dangers and distress. Christ here wants to exhort and console us, that we may be reconciled to our lot and not be too alarmed or let the devil subdue us so easily and make us despair and lose courage.

From these and similar words of Christ we should learn to know the Lord Christ aright, to develop a more cordial and comforting confidence in him. We are to learn to pay more regard to his word than to anything else which may confront our eyes, ears, and other senses.

For if I am a Christian and hold to him, I always know that he is talking to me. Here and elsewhere I learn that all his words are intended to comfort me. Yes, all he says, does, and thinks are nothing but friendly and consoling words and works. To this end he promises to send his disciples and the Christians the Holy Spirit, whom he calls the Comforter.

Sermons on the Gospel of St. John (1537)
LW 24, 12-13

HOPE

For through the Spirit, by faith, we eagerly wait
for the hope of righteousness.
—*Galatians 5:5*

THEREFORE WHEN I TAKE HOLD OF CHRIST AS I HAVE BEEN taught by faith in the word of God, and when I believe in him with the full confidence of my heart—something that cannot happen without the will—then I am righteous through this knowledge, then immediately the devil comes and exerts himself to extinguish my faith with his tricks, his lies, errors and heresies, violence, tyranny, and murder.

Then my battling hope grasps what faith has commanded; it becomes vigorous and conquers the devil, who attacks faith. When he has been conquered, there follow peace and joy in the Holy Spirit. Faith and hope are scarcely distinguishable; and yet there is some difference between them.

Therefore faith is like dialectic, which conceives the idea of all the things that are to be believed; and hope is like rhetoric, which develops, urges, persuades, and exhorts to steadiness, so that faith does not collapse in temptation but keeps the word and holds firmly to it.

Lectures on Galatians (1535)
LW 27, 23-24

Hoping against hope, [Abraham] believed that he would
become "the father of many nations."
—*Romans 4:18*

Truly devout people have nothing dearer and more precious in the whole world than this doctrine. Those who hold to this know what the whole world does not know, namely, that sin and death, as well as other calamities and evils, both physical and spiritual, work out for the good of the elect. They also know that God is present most closely when he seems to be farthest away, and that he is most merciful and most the Savior when he seems most to be wrathful and to punish and condemn. They know that they have eternal righteousness, for which they look in hope as an utterly certain possession [Gal. 5:5], laid up in heaven, when they are most aware of the terrors of sin and death; and that they are the lords of everything when they seem to be the poorest of all, according to the words, "as having nothing, and yet possessing everything" (2 Cor. 6:10). This is what Scripture calls gaining comfort through hope. But this art is not learned without frequent and great trials.

Lectures on Galatians (1535)
LW 27, 27

The saying is sure and worthy of full acceptance.
For to this end we toil and struggle, because we have
our hope set on the living God, who is the Savior
of all people, especially of those who believe.
—1 Timothy 4:9-10

This firm hope that we have makes us quick to work and to bear reproach. This statement is sure because we have this man who will yet come. So we work, exercise godliness, do our tasks, observe all things, that the glory of God may grow and the kingdom of God may be spread.

As to our hardships: then we not only work but also suffer. In both areas we practice the word, actively and passively. Why this? Because our hope rests on a living God. We do not place our hope in the world. We do not work or suffer reproach so that we experience the favor, wealth, and high positions of the world. We do not hope in an imaginary god. Such are the gods of hypocrites, who make up gods for themselves with their false religion. They work and suffer in vain, because their hopes lie in an imaginary god.

Our hope truly is in a real God. Those who hope in God know for certain that their works and suffering please God. They most certainly experience mercy and grace from God. The person, then, who has this confidence acts the more freely and endures everything, because he or she always has this confidence in pleasing God.

"Lectures on 1 Timothy" (1527-28)
LW 28, 325

"And I will put enmity between you and the woman,
and between your offspring and hers; he will strike
your head, and you will strike his heel."
—Genesis 3:15

T his is the text that made Adam and Eve alive and brought them back from death into the life, which they had lost through sin. Nevertheless, the life is one hoped for rather than one already possessed. Similarly, Paul also often says (1 Cor. 15:31): "Daily we die." Although we do not wish to call the life we live here a death, nevertheless it surely is nothing else than a continuous journey toward death. Just as a person infected with a plague has already started to die when the infection has begun, so—because of sin and death, the punishment for sin—this life can no longer properly be called life after it has been infected by sin. Right from our mother's womb we begin to die.

Through Baptism we are restored to a life of hope, or rather to a hope of life. This is the true life, which is lived before God. Before we come to it, we are in the midst of death. We die and decay in the earth, just as other dead bodies do, as though there were no other life anywhere. Yet we who believe in Christ have the hope that on the last day we shall be revived for eternal life.

Lectures on Genesis (1535-36)
LW 1, 196

A broken and contrite heart, O God, you will not despise.
—Psalm 51:17b

This is a description of God that is full of comfort: that in his true form God is a God who loves the afflicted, has mercy upon the humbled, forgives the fallen, and revives the drooping. How can any more pleasant picture be painted of God? This verse rejects all other acts of worship and all works and simply calls us back to trust alone in the mercy and kindness of God, so that we believe that God is favorably disposed to us even when we seem to ourselves to be forsaken and distressed.

Thus when Nathan denounced David (2 Sam. 12:7): "You are that man of death," David was humbled and undertook this sacrifice. Then when he heard (2 Sam. 12:13): "You shall not die," he completed the sacrifice. In the midst of wrath he acquired hope in mercy; in the midst of a feeling of death he acquired a hope in life. From that experience this verse was born, by which we are taught about a sacrifice acceptable to God, namely, to hope for life and grace amid death and the wrath of God.

125

This theology must be learned through experience. Without experience it cannot be understood that the "poor in spirit" (Matt. 5:3) should know that they are in grace when they most feel the wrath of God, that in despair they should keep their hope in mercy, and in smugness they should keep their fear of God. As another passage says (Ps. 147:11): "The Lord takes pleasure in those who fear him, in those who hope in his steadfast love."

Commentary on "Psalm 51" (1532)
LW 12, 406

CHRIST THE KING

The LORD says to my lord,"Sit at my right hand."
—Psalm 110:1a

ONE WORD EXALTS HIM TO THE POSITION OF A GLORIOUS KING!
Not over that beggarly palace in Jerusalem or the imperial
throne of Babylon or Rome or Constantinople or the whole
earth—which would indeed represent tremendous power. Not
merely king of the heavens, the stars, and anything else that the
eye can see! This is something far higher and more important,
for it means: "Sit next to me on the exalted throne upon which
I sit, and be my equal!"

To sit next to him—at his right hand, not at his feet—
means to possess the very majesty and power that is called
divine. Surely, by this one short word Christ is raised from the
earth and exalted above all the heavens, as St. Paul says (Phil.
2:9-10), and becomes a king inconceivably glorious and of
unspeakable power. He is not merely a king who rules over all
people, but one who is above the heavens, angels, and anything
else that is subject to God.

Commentary on "Psalm 110" (1535)
LW 13, 233-34

*[Jesus Christ] has gone into heaven and is
at the right hand of God, with angels, authorities,
and powers made subject to him.*
—*1 Peter 3:22*

This is really an extraordinary kingdom. This king sits above at the right hand of God, where he is invisible, an eternal, immortal person. But his people are here below on earth in this miserable, mortal condition, subjected to death and any kind of mishap that a person may meet on earth.

But this Lord Christ sits above at the right hand of God, having a kingdom of life, peace, joy, and redemption from all evil, not a kingdom of death, sorrow, and misery. Therefore it must follow that his own will not remain subject to death, anxiety, fear, spiritual conflict, and suffering. They will be snatched from death or the grave and all misery. They will live with him beyond sin and evil after he has made them alive again in body and soul.

He illustrates this in his own person. He became a human being and condescended to the miserable level of our present nature in order to begin his kingdom in us by personally sharing all human weakness and trouble. For this reason he also had to die. But if he was meant to be Lord and king of all creation, sitting at the right hand of God, he could not remain under the conditions of death and suffering. By God's power he had to break through death and the grave and everything else, so that he might seat himself at the place where he can work all these things in us and grant them to us.

*Commentary on "Psalm 110" (1535)
LW 13, 240-41*

"When he ascended on high he made captivity
itself a captive; he gave gifts to his people."
—*Ephesians 4:8b*

Behold the glory of this king! It surpasses all that is glorious and powerful, whether in heaven or on earth. He is a different Lord, unlike those who have land and people, cities and castles, silver and gold, body and goods. He is Lord and king of eternal possessions that are peculiar to God, such as peace and joy and the immeasurable wealth of eternal righteousness and life. Of course, he also holds in his hands all that pertains to this temporal life, whatever there is of power and authority. He can do with it as he sees fit. Hence all princes and lords are subject to him; they cannot reach beyond the limits he has set for them. But as Psalm 110 shows, it is of special importance that the devil, death, and sin have been put under his feet unconditionally.

At this point we must mention the faith that takes hold of the king. We must learn to see Christ thus and to believe it with certainty, so that he becomes such a Lord for us also. For he is not someone who lolls in heaven and has fun with the angels. He exercises his authority and government vigorously and under all conditions by controlling the hearts of all. He does truly govern, lead, save, protect, and preserve his Christendom. All who believe in him and call upon him certainly receive the gifts described by St. Paul, who cites Psalm 68:18 in Ephesians 4:8 to show that Christ ascended on high and seated himself at the right hand of God in order to give people such divine gifts.

Commentary on "Psalm 110" (1535)
LW 13, 241

Your solemn processions are seen, O God, the processions
of my God, my King, into the sanctuary.
—Psalm 68:24

God's "processions" represent his work, which is steadfast love and faithfulness. Thus we read in Psalm 25:10: "All the paths of the Lord are steadfast love and faithfulness." However, it requires great skill to recognize God's work and to let him work in us, so that all our work will in the end be God's and not our own. This is the proper celebration of the Sabbath, to rest from our own works and to be full of God's works. All this is effected in us through faith, which teaches that we count for naught and our work no less. This is what the psalmist has in mind when he says: "Thy processions are seen and recognized." And the words "my God, my king" point to Christ, who is our king according to his human nature, and who is God from eternity.

We cannot say "My god and my king" unless we regard God with the eyes of faith, not only as a god, not only as a king, but as our god and our king, as the god and king of our salvation. Neither is it possible to recognize the ways and works of God in the absence of that faith. Faith renders him my god and my king, and brings me to a realization that all my works are, after all, not mine but God's.

129

Commentary on "Psalm 68" (1521)
LW 13, 25-26

In your majesty ride forth victoriously in behalf of truth,
humility and righteousness; let your right hand
display awesome deeds.
—Psalm 45:4 (NIV)

Therefore rouse yourself. Do not give in to evils, but go forth more boldly against them. Hold on. Do not be disheartened either by contempt or ingratitude within or by agitation and raging without. It is in sorrow, when we are the closest to despair, that hope rises the highest. So today, when there is the greatest contempt and weariness with the Word, the true glory of the Word begins.

Therefore we should learn to understand this verse as speaking of invisible progress and success. Our king enjoys success and good fortune even though you do not see it. Moreover, it would not be expedient for us to see this success, for then we would be puffed up. Now, however, he raises us up through faith and gives us hope. Even though we see no fruit of the Word, still we can be certain that fruit will not be wanting but will certainly follow. We should not be discouraged when we look at present circumstances that disturb us, but we should much rather look at Christ's promises. He is the kind of king who will have success, steadfastness, and victory—if not in this place and time, then at another time and place. This splendor and success is clearer than all the stars, even though we do not see it.

Commentary on "Psalm 45" (1532)
LW 12, 220-21

BIBLIOGRAPHY

Doberstein, John W., ed. *Minister's Prayer Book.* Philadelphia: Muhlenberg Press, n.d.

Lutheran Book of Worship. Minneapolis: Augsburg Publishing House, 1978.

The Lutheran Hymnal. St. Louis: Concordia Publishing House, 1941.

Lutheran Worship. St. Louis: Concordia Publishing House, 1982.

Pelikan, Jaroslav, and Helmut Lehmann, eds. *Luther's Works.* American Edition. Philadelphia and St. Louis: Fortress Press and Concordia Publishing House, 1955-1984.

Plass, Ewald M., ed. *What Luther Says.* An Anthology. St. Louis: Concordia Publishing House, 1959.

Tappert, Theodore G., ed. and trans. *Luther: Letters of Spiritual Counsel.* Vol. 18 of The Library of Christian Classics. Philadelphia: The Westminster Press, 1955.

OTHER RESOURCES FROM AUGSBURG

These Words upon Your Heart edited by Paul Ofstedal
160 pages, 0-8066-4421-4

Quotations from the writings of classic spiritual writers provide
the starting point for the devotions included in this book. Each
of the contributors has written devotions based on one classic
author.

Psalms: The Prayer Book of the Bible by Dietrich Bonhoeffer
86 pages, 0-8066-1439-0

In this introduction, Bonhoeffer discusses the various types of
Psalms and how they can be used to enrich our prayer life.

Faith, The Yes of the Heart by Grace Brame
192 pages, 0-8066-3805-2

In this rich and rewarding theology of spirituality, author
Grace Brame draws from the insights of leading spiritual
thinkers. This is a book to inspire, to give courage, and to
open the reader to the possibilities of trusting love.

My Conversations with Martin Luther by Timothy Lull
160 pages, 0-8066-3898-2

In this richly imagined book, Timothy Lull engages in a
series of dialogues with the great church reformer. He also
offers suggestions on how you can begin your own conversations with Martin Luther.

Available wherever books are sold.
To order these books directly, contact:
1-800-328-4648 • www.augsburgfortress.org
Augsburg Fortress, Publishers
P.O. Box 1209, Minneapolis, MN 55440-1209